THE LIZZIE BORDEN "AXE MURDER" TRIAL

A Headline Court Case

Headline Court Cases

The Andersonville Prison Civil War Crimes Trial
A Headline Court Case
0-7660-1386-3

The John Brown Slavery Revolt Trial
A Headline Court Case
0-7660-1385-5

The Lindbergh Baby Kidnapping Trial
A Headline Court Case
0-7660-1389-8

The Lizzie Borden "Axe Murder" Trial
A Headline Court Case
0-7660-1422-3

The Nuremberg Nazi War Crimes Trials
A Headline Court Case
0-7660-1384-7

The Sacco and Vanzetti Controversial Murder Trial
A Headline Court Case
0-7660-1387-1

The Salem Witchcraft Trials
A Headline Court Case
0-7660-1383-9

The Scopes Monkey Trial
A Headline Court Case
0-7660-1388-X

THE LIZZIE BORDEN "AXE MURDER" TRIAL

A Headline Court Case

Joan Axelrod-Contrada

Enslow Publishers, Inc.

40 Industrial Road   PO Box 38
Box 398   Aldershot
Berkeley Heights, NJ 07922   Hants GU12 6BP
USA   UK

http://www.enslow.com

Library of Congress Cataloging-in-Publication Data

Axelrod-Contrada, Joan.
    The Lizzie Borden "Axe murder" trial: a headline court case / Joan
Axelrod-Contrada.
        p. cm. — (Headline court cases)
    Includes bibliographical references and index.
    Summary: Examines one of the most celebrated murder trials in United
States history, in which Lizzie Borden was accused of killing her father
and stepmother with an axe.
    ISBN 0-7660-1422-3
    1. Borden, Lizzie, 1860–1927—Trials, litigation, etc.—Juvenile
literature. 2. Trials (Murder)—Massachusetts—New Bedford—Juvenile
literature. [1. Borden, Lizzie, 1860–1927—Trials, litigation, etc.
2. Trials (Murder)] I. Title. II. Series.
    KF223.B6 A98 2000
    345.73'02523—dc21   00-008136

Printed in the United States of America

10 9 8 7 6 5 4 3 2 1

To Our Readers:
All Internet addresses in this book were active and appropriate when we went to press.
Any comments can be sent by e-mail to Comments@enslow.com or to the address on
the back cover.

Photo Credits: The Fall River Historical Society, pp. 3, 10, 17, 22, 27, 34, 44,
53, 58, 67, 70, 76, 83, 88, 96, 101

Cover Photo: The Fall River Historical Society

Contents

Author's Note

So much has been written about Lizzie Borden that at times the information found in different sources can be contradictory. I have woven together the information found in a variety of sources, making every effort to maintain consistency while avoiding any graphic descriptions of the crime.

chapter one

A TERRIBLE CRIME

FALL RIVER, MA—One August morning in 1892, in Fall River, Massachusetts, thirty-two-year-old Lizzie Borden called to her maid Bridget "Maggie" Sullivan.

"Maggie!" she cried. "Come down!"

"What's the matter?" the maid asked.

"Come down here! Father's dead; someone came in and killed him."[1]

The twenty-six-year-old maid from Ireland ran down the back stairs of the wooden house at 92 Second Street. Lizzie Borden's father, one of the wealthiest men in Fall River, had last been seen resting in the downstairs sitting room. Bridget Sullivan turned to check on him.

"Don't go in there," Borden said. "Go and get the doctor. Run."[2]

Bridget Sullivan rushed to the home of Dr. Seabury Bowen, but he was not there. So, she left a message with his wife and returned home. Lizzie Borden then ordered her to find Alice Russell, a friend who lived a few blocks away.

Frenzied Comings and Goings

Next-door neighbor Adelaide Churchill noticed Bridget

Sullivan's frenzied comings and goings and called out her window to Lizzie Borden. Was anything the matter?

"Oh, Mrs. Churchill, please come over!" Lizzie Borden called back. "Someone has killed father!"[3]

"Where is your mother?" Mrs. Churchill asked, referring to Lizzie Borden's stepmother.

Lizzie Borden replied that her stepmother had gotten a note and was visiting a sick friend. Mrs. Churchill and her handyman went for help.

At 11:15 A.M., the Fall River Police Department received word of the murder. It was Thursday morning, August 4, 1892.

Bridget Sullivan returned home with Alice Russell. The maid then asked Lizzie Borden where she was at the time of the disturbance.

"I was in the yard," Lizzie Borden replied.[4] She would later tell others that she was in the barn or the hayloft at the time.

A Sunday School Teacher

Lizzie Borden, a Sunday school teacher and member of the Women's Christian Temperance Union, came from a wealthy, though troubled, family. Christened Lizzie rather than Elizabeth, she was only two years old when her mother, Sarah Morse Borden, died. Lizzie's older sister, Emma, who was twelve at the time, became like a mother to Lizzie.

Their father, Andrew Borden, was a tall, thin, conservative man known for his thrift and sharp business instincts. In 1865, when Lizzie was five years old, he married Abby

Durfee Gray, a woman in her late thirties. The daughter of a tin peddler, Abby Gray lacked the social status of the wealthier Bordens. Emma and Lizzie did not approve of their new stepmother.

A Troubled History

Household tensions increased in 1887, when Andrew Borden bought a portion of a house for his wife's half sister. Lizzie and Emma Borden saw the purchase as proof of their father's loyalty to his new wife over his daughters. Lizzie Borden stopped calling her stepmother "mother," choosing instead the more formal "Mrs. Borden."

The Borden parents and daughters split into camps divided by locked doors and separate stairways. The daughters called Bridget Sullivan "Maggie," the name of their former maid. The parents called her "Bridget." The Borden daughters avoided meeting their father and stepmother at the dinner table.

Of the two daughters, Lizzie had the stronger personality.[5] She was tight-lipped, proud, and perpetually moody.[6] On the day of the murders, her sister was away visiting friends in Fairhaven, Massachusetts.

The Doctor

When the doctor arrived at the Bordens' house on Second Street, he was shocked by what he saw. Seventy-year-old bank president Andrew J. Borden lay dead in the sitting room, the victim of a horrific crime. From the size of the wounds, the doctor concluded that the blows had been delivered by a sharp instrument such as an axe or a hatchet.

(An axe is a cutting tool or weapon with a heavy-bladed head attached to a handle. A hatchet is an axe with a short handle that can be used with one hand.)

The doctor left the house for a short while to send a telegram to Emma Borden asking her to come home. Word of Andrew Borden's murder spread, attracting a crowd to

Andrew Borden's body was found by his daughter Lizzie on the morning of August 4, 1892.

Second Street. The women inside the house hovered over Lizzie Borden, fanning her and applying cold compresses to her head. Once again, someone asked about Abby Borden. Bridget Sullivan would later testify that Lizzie Borden asked her to look for her stepmother, saying she thought she had heard her return.

The maid, though, feared that the killer was still in the house and refused to go upstairs alone. Adelaide Churchill volunteered to accompany her. The two women discovered Abby Borden's dead body lying on the floor in the upstairs guestroom. The pillowcases were perfectly straight, the way she had left them. Nothing had been taken. There were no signs of burglary. Adelaide Churchill rushed downstairs.

"Is there another?" Miss Russell asked.

"Yes, she is up there," Mrs. Churchill replied.[7]

Dr. Bowen returned from his errand and, upon hearing the news, examined the second body. He and Alice Russell searched in vain for the note about the sick call that Abby Borden had supposedly made. Alice Russell suggested that perhaps Abby Borden had thrown the note into the fire.

The Police

The police soon arrived on the scene. Due to the power and prestige of the Borden name, they proceeded cautiously. No one immediately examined the clothing of Lizzie Borden or Bridget Sullivan. Fingerprinting was not yet used in Fall River.[8]

One police officer apologetically asked Lizzie Borden if there were any hatchets or axes in the house. Yes, she replied; there were both. Bridget Sullivan led the officer down to the basement, where he found several axes and hatchets. Gray hairs were stuck to one. Another had a freshly broken handle.

Another officer went out to the barn loft to check for footprints. He saw nothing but decided to perform an experiment. He put his hand down to see if it made any impression. It did. From that, he concluded that no one had been in the barn loft that day. Lizzie Borden's alibi, her reason to explain why she could not have committed the crime, was now in dispute.

Cool Demeanor

The medical examiner checked the bodies and concluded that over an hour had passed between the two murders.[9] Abby Borden had been killed first. Whoever committed the crime had left $85.65 in Andrew Borden's wallet. Officers searched Abby Borden's pocketbook and sewing box for the note about the sick call but found nothing.

Another officer approached Lizzie Borden. Because of the brutality of the crime, he offered to come back later. Lizzie Borden replied that she could speak to him just as well then as any other time. The officer was struck by her cool demeanor.[10]

Assistant Marshal John Fleet, whose position was equivalent to that of deputy police chief, also spoke to Lizzie Borden. (A marshal is a high-ranking officer in the police, military, or judicial system.) First, he asked her who was in the house that morning. She said her father, stepmother,

Bridget Sullivan, and an uncle, John Vinnicum Morse, visiting from out of town, were there.[11]

Then Fleet asked if Lizzie Borden thought that either her uncle or the maid could have committed the crime. No, she replied; her uncle had gone to visit relatives, and the maid had spent the morning washing windows.

"Do you know of anyone who might have killed your father and mother?" the deputy marshal pressed on.

"She is not my *mother*, sir," Lizzie Borden replied pointedly. "She is my stepmother. My mother died when I was a child."[12]

Fleet took Lizzie Borden's response as an expression of ill will toward her stepmother. It was a remark that would echo through the trial.[13]

chapter two

AMERICA IN THE 1890s

THE VICTORIAN AGE— America was shocked by the idea that a respectable woman such as Lizzie Borden might actually have killed her parents. Women in the Victorian era (the time from 1837–1901 when Queen Victoria ruled over Great Britain) rarely, if ever, committed murder. For an upper-class woman to stab her victims to death was rarer still. A proper woman like Lizzie Borden would surely use a gentler means of destruction, such as poison, or so people thought at the time.[1]

In the late nineteenth century in New England, class distinctions mattered a great deal. Writer Mark Twain coined the phrase the Gilded Age to describe an America covered with a thin layer of gold—more attractive on the surface than down below. Beneath the glittery wealth of the 1890s, however, lay poverty and unrest.

Between 1865 and 1900, over 12 million immigrants arrived in the United States.[2] Many headed for the factories and mills of the industrial Northeast.

Resentment against and anger toward immigrants ran high. While some newcomers like Andrew Carnegie gained great wealth, many others lived in poverty. Children worked long hours in airless factories. The nation became divided into natives and foreigners, old-timers and newcomers.

Many old-time families hired immigrants as servants. Newly manufactured goods, too, freed middle-class women from long hours of spinning, sewing, and churning. Wealthy women had little to do at home but iron their handkerchiefs and perhaps do some fancy needlepoint.[3]

A Woman's Place

Women's legal status in the 1890s was mixed. Although they were still unable to vote or sit on juries, women had gained some property rights and contractual rights. A wife was no longer merely her husband's possession. Laws concerning women, however, varied from state to state and court to court. Often it took a landmark court case or a change in state law—or both—for instance, for a woman to be able to practice law.[4] During the Victorian era, individuals interested in becoming lawyers either attended law school or trained as an apprentice before taking a state bar exam in order to practice law.

A Landmark Case

One landmark case occurred after the state of Illinois refused to admit Myra Colby Bradwell to the bar association, a group of lawyers, judges, law students, and law teachers, simply because she was a married woman. In

1873, the United States Supreme Court ruled that because Bradwell lacked the right to make contracts as a married woman, she should be denied admission to the bar. By the time the Supreme Court reached its decision, however, the state of Illinois had already passed a law giving all persons, regardless of gender, the freedom to select their own occupation. So, the Supreme Court's decision was never applied to married women in Illinois.[5] In Massachusetts, too, women were able to become lawyers by 1892.[6]

Still, the tradition of man as the protector and woman as the protected continued. A court ruling in 1875 justified protective labor laws for women by stating, "The law of nature destines and qualifies the female sex for the bearing and nurture of the children of our race and for the custody of the homes of the world in love and honor."[7]

A woman's place was still in the home. Women would have to wait until 1920 to win the right to vote. Old-fashioned notions of gender prevailed. Three-quarters of all American women in the late nineteenth century married between the ages of nineteen and twenty-five.[8] Those who did not were seen as spinsters—women who were single and had passed the common age for marrying—and were expected to retire to their homes and engage in charitable pursuits.

Delicate Creatures

Victorian ladies were generally considered fragile and delicate creatures. Magazines of the day observed that women made up for their lack of strength with a heightened sense of morality.[9] Suffragists, supporters of a woman's right to vote, argued that women should be allowed to vote because they were morally superior to men.

While women were still expected to get married and have children, some went off to the new women's colleges, campaigned for social change, or joined the professional world. Settlement houses, community centers for the neighborhood poor, provided job opportunities for idealistic young people with a sense of adventure. Jane Addams, for example, founded Hull House in Chicago.

Lizzie Borden, however, lacked such ambitions. She left high school before graduation, engaging in various charities that befitted a woman of her class. She became head of the local hospital's Fruit and Flower Mission and taught Sunday school to the children of Fall River's Chinese laundrymen.[10] Lizzie Borden, however, seemed dissatisfied with her life of leisure and good works.[11]

Little Merriment

Fall River offered little in the way of entertainment. As one writer observed, "It was the Naughty Nineties in everywhere but dour Fall River."[12]

Lizzie Borden did not get along with her stepmother, Abby Borden (shown here). The relationship between the two became strained when Andrew Borden bought a portion of a house for his wife's half sister.

Fall River was a typical New England mill town, made prosperous by the water power of the Quequechan River and an ample supply of immigrant labor. Protestant old-timers like the Bordens held a higher social position than the largely Catholic and Jewish newcomers from Ireland, Russia, Portugal, and elsewhere. The Borden name was a social advantage. Everyone in Fall River knew the Bordens and other leading citizens at least by sight.[13]

A Well-Known Family

The Borden family's roots in New England dated back to the 1600s, with some members of the family prospering more than others. Andrew Borden's father was one of the less fortunate ones—a fish peddler. Andrew Borden vowed to do better.[14]

In the course of his career, Andrew Borden rose from undertaker to bank president. Through smart business practices and investment in real estate, he accumulated a fortune worth over a quarter of a million dollars. He easily could have afforded a house in the wealthy section of Fall River known as The Hill. Instead, he chose to economize and live downtown.

In 1843, Andrew Borden married Sarah Morse, a farm girl. The couple had three daughters, only two of whom survived. On July 19, 1860, their youngest daughter, christened Lizzie Andrew Borden, was born. That same year, Abraham Lincoln ran for president and won. Sarah Borden died in March 1863.

A Second Wife

One day in 1865, Andrew Borden walked home from church with thirty-seven-year-old Abby Durfee Gray. Shortly thereafter, he proposed marriage. Some skeptics believed that Andrew Borden married his second wife merely to get a free housekeeper and babysitter.[15]

Emma and Lizzie looked down on their stepmother.[16] Abby Borden had a much closer relationship with her half sister, Sarah Whitehead. Because Sarah Whitehead and her husband, George, could not afford to buy the house where they lived, they faced eviction. Abby Borden persuaded Andrew to buy the property in her name with the understanding that the Whiteheads be allowed to live there rent-free.

The Borden daughters saw this purchase as proof that their father favored his wife over them. Andrew Borden tried to calm his daughters by buying them another house worth three thousand dollars. The daughters, though, lost interest in this house, and returned it to their father. They continued to resent their stepmother.[17]

Frugal or Miserly

Andrew Borden was either frugal or miserly, depending on one's point of view. Nevertheless, he sometimes showed uncharacteristic generosity toward his youngest daughter, buying her expensive gifts such as a diamond ring and a sealskin cape. He even paid for her to go on a grand tour of Europe in 1890. She, in turn, gave him her high school ring as a symbol of the bond between them. He wore the ring on his pinky finger until the day he died.

Yet Andrew and Lizzie Borden also had their disagreements. Lizzie Borden wanted to live on The Hill, not in a shabby house near the factories.[18] She dressed stylishly and wore her auburn hair in the style of the day. Her prominent pale eyes photographed well, and she enjoyed having her picture taken. Lizzie Borden liked being noticed.[19] Andrew Borden, on the other hand, dressed somberly in black suits year round.

Unlike his cousins who lived in luxury on The Hill, Andrew Borden clearly lived below his means. He shunned modern conveniences, which had become commonplace even among middle-class families in 1892. Instead of running water, the Bordens had a pump in the sink room. Rather than opt for gas or electric lights, they held on to their kerosene lamps. The house on Second Street even lacked a modern bathroom. No space was wasted on hallways. Rooms simply opened into one another. For privacy, the Bordens designed their own intricate system of separate stairways and locked doors.

On Tuesday, August 2, 1892, the Bordens had leftover fish for dinner. In those days, before modern refrigeration, food often spoiled in the summer. On Wednesday, August 3, 1892, the day before the murders, everyone in the Borden household complained of stomach problems.[20]

Fear of Poison

Abby Borden was convinced she had been poisoned. Her frugal husband, though, thought it was unnecessary for her to see a doctor. Over his objections, she went to see Dr.

Bowen anyway. He attributed her problems to spoiled food and sent her home. Andrew Borden ungraciously told the doctor that he would not pay any bill for the visit.

On the evening before the murders, Lizzie Borden, too, spoke ominously about poison. She complained to her friend Alice Russell that she felt depressed. "I think our milk might be poisoned," she said.[21] Their barn, she added, had been broken into twice. Alice Russell blamed the burglaries on boys looking for pigeons.

But Lizzie Borden persisted, saying the house, too, had been burglarized. She was referring to an incident the previous summer when Andrew Borden had reported that someone had broken into his home and stolen his gold watch and various other items. A few days later, he called the police to call off the investigation. Officials at the stationhouse suspected that the robber was someone in his own household.[22] Now, a year later, on the night before the murders, Lizzie Borden told Alice Russell she feared that someone might harm her family.

The Uncle

Meanwhile, John Vinnicum Morse had come to visit. The brother of Andrew Borden's first wife, Morse had gone out West as a young man to make his fortune. He found success in Iowa, first as a farmer, then as a horse trader. Two years before the murders, he returned East to establish a horse-farm in Swansea, Massachusetts, where Andrew Borden kept his own horses. Andrew Borden liked his brother-in-law and valued his advice on business matters.[23]

This picture of Lizzie Borden was taken in 1877 when she was seventeen years old, fifteen years before her father and stepmother were murdered.

Lizzie Borden, though, had a chilly relationship with her uncle, whom she suspected of being involved in the transfer of the house to her stepmother five years earlier.[24] Lizzie Borden refused to see her uncle when he came to visit.

A Fateful Morning

On Thursday morning, August 4, 1892—the day of the murders—Bridget Sullivan prepared the family a breakfast that included leftover mutton (an inexpensive cut of meat from a grown sheep rather than a young lamb) and johnnycakes (pancakes made out of cornmeal). Lizzie Borden stayed in her room. Once her uncle left the house at about 8:45 A.M., she came downstairs, saying she would fix her own breakfast. She wanted only coffee and cookies. Her father left the house around 9:00 A.M. to make his business calls downtown. Abby Borden instructed Bridget Sullivan to wash the windows, then went upstairs to straighten up the guestroom where Uncle John had spent the night. She never lived to see the noon hour.

Andrew Borden returned home around 10:40 A.M. and went to lie down on the sofa in the sitting room. Finished with the outside windows, Bridget Sullivan began on the inside ones. Lizzie Borden came into the dining room to iron her handkerchiefs.

Bridget Sullivan later remembered Lizzie Borden telling her, "There is a cheap sale of dress goods at Sargent's, at eight cents a yard." To which, she replied: "I am going to have one [a dress]."[25]

But the day did not go according to plan. Bridget

Sullivan went up to her attic bedroom to rest. The clock struck eleven. About fifteen minutes later, she heard Lizzie Borden's cries for help.

News of the Murders

Before long, the news would hit the streets. Andrew and Abby Borden were dead. If such prominent citizens could be murdered in the privacy of their home, then no one was safe. People worried that the killer might strike again.

Fall River's daily newspapers scurried to meet their deadlines. The first edition of *The Daily Herald* came out Thursday afternoon at 2:15. Within minutes, it sold out. In keeping with the sensationalistic journalism of the day, the headlines graphically depicted the brutality of the crime.

Hundreds of people left work and rushed to Second Street to hear the latest on the crime. Businesses shut down because many employees never returned from their lunch hour. By 5:00 that evening, a new edition of the *Herald* hit the streets with the headline: "A Deep Mystery: Hundreds in Front of the Borden Homestead Discussing the Murder— Miss Borden Has Not the Least Suspicion of the Guilty Parties—Police Scouring the Town."[26]

Another Newspaper

Fall River's *Daily Globe* competed with the *Herald* for readers. The self-appointed defender of the working class, the *Daily Globe* delighted in taking on Fall River's rich and powerful. Unlike many newspapers of the time, it was skeptical from the start of Lizzie Borden's innocence. The

Daily Globe speculated on a motive for the murders: greed. Under Massachusetts law, Abby Borden would inherit one-third of her husband's estate if he died first, thus depriving the daughters of some of their father's fortune.[27]

Newspaper reporters from around the nation flocked to Fall River to cover the Borden murders.

Henry Trickey of *The Boston Globe* was one of the most flamboyant. He would later disgrace his newspaper by filing a false story based on information bought by a freelance detective. Trickey's article claimed that Lizzie Borden had once been pregnant. *The Boston Globe* rushed the story into print without verifying it. The story turned out to be totally false.[28]

Purchase of Poison

Police officers, meanwhile, made the rounds of area pharmacies to see if anyone had purchased poison recently in keeping with the fears of Abby and Lizzie Borden. Pharmacist Eli Bence told a shocking story. A woman he identified as Lizzie Borden had come into his store on Wednesday asking for prussic acid, a poisonous colorless liquid with the smell of peach blossoms or bitter almonds. The pharmacist remembered her saying that she needed it to clean a sealskin cape. He turned down her request, saying that she needed a prescription.

The police tried to keep the results of the investigation secret, but it was no use. On Friday, the front-page headline of Fall River's *Daily Globe* screamed, "What Did Lizzie Want of Poison?"[29]

That evening, Emma and Lizzie Borden offered a five-thousand-dollar reward in the *The Daily Herald* for information leading to the arrest and conviction of anyone responsible for the death of their father and stepmother.

Overnight, townspeople and journalists turned into amateur detectives, puzzling over questions like, "Who could have committed such a crime? What was the motive? How had the murderer escaped unnoticed?"[30] Everyone, it seemed, had their own theory about the murders. Police officers patrolled the curious crowds in front of the Borden house on Second Street.

Townspeople's Suspicions

Dozens of letters urging the arrest of Bridget Sullivan poured into the Fall River police station. The courteous and respectful attitude shown to a "lady" like Lizzie Borden did not extend to the maid, Bridget Sullivan.[31]

Uncle John Morse, too, came under suspicion. On Friday, August 5, the day after the murders, when he left the house to mail a letter, hundreds of angry people mobbed him.[32] A police officer rescued him and brought him back to safety. Morse protested his innocence to the press. The relatives he was visiting at the time of the murders confirmed his alibi.

Amateur investigators also focused on the question of the missing note summoning Abby Borden to visit a sick friend. A New York newspaper offered a five-hundred-dollar reward for proof of the note, but no one came forward. The question of whether Abby Borden ever left the house that morning remained a mystery.

The police, meanwhile, investigated the leads flooding into the stationhouse. One man reported seeing a "wild-eyed" man on Second Street about an hour or two before the murders. The wild eyes, it turned out, were caused by a simple hangover. Others accused a Portuguese worker of committing the murders. The Portuguese worker, though, was actually a Swede with an alibi. Reports of unknown buggy drivers, gypsy horse traders, and suspicious Frenchmen, too, proved to be dead ends.

Police Search

Police searched the Borden house once again on the day after the murders. Intent on finding the bloodstained garments worn by the killer, the police once again came up empty.

Also, on Friday, August 5, 1892, Hiram Harrington, a Borden relative by marriage, spoke freely with newspaper reporters. Harrington was married to Andrew Borden's sister, Laurana. According to Andrew Borden, Harrington, a mere blacksmith, was unworthy of his sister.

Shortly before the murders occurred, Lizzie Borden told Bridget Sullivan (shown here) that she was going shopping. Fifteen minutes after Sullivan went to her attic bedroom to rest, she heard Lizzie Borden's cries for help.

Harrington told reporters that the Borden daughters had been feuding with their father and stepmother for nearly ten years. Lizzie Borden, he said, was an uppity and domineering woman who had often spoken bitterly about her father. On the day of the murders, he said, she showed no signs of emotion.[33]

Despite other reports to the contrary, this cool, calm, composed image of Lizzie Borden haunted her forever.[34]

A Private Funeral

On Saturday, August 6, 1892, the daughters held private funeral services in their home for Abby and Andrew Borden. A wreath of ivy lay on Andrew's body, a bouquet of white roses and ferns on Abby's. Thousands of people lined the streets to catch a glimpse of the funeral procession to the cemetery. Lizzie Borden emerged from her house leaning on the arm of the undertaker.

Police searched the house yet another time, combing it from attic to cellar. Again, they found no clues. On the way out, the police asked Lizzie Borden to turn over the clothes she wore on the morning of the murders. She surrendered a blue silk two-piece dress and starched white underskirt.

Lizzie Borden as a Suspect

The Fall River Police Department had become increasingly convinced that Lizzie Borden was involved in the murders.[35] But, to arrest her, Marshal Rufus B. Hilliard, whose position was equivalent to police chief, needed hard evidence, which he did not have. Concerned about the sometimes unruly crowds outside the Borden house, he called the district attorney, Hosea Knowlton, for advice. (A district attorney is the attorney who conducts criminal cases on behalf of the state or the people, for the local area.) The district attorney offered to take the early evening train from New Bedford to Fall River to meet with the marshal. The case against Lizzie Borden would be brought by the Commonwealth of Massachusetts. While waiting for the district attorney, the marshal met with the mayor of Fall River.

The mayor and the marshal decided to set out immediately for Second Street to urge members of the Borden household to stay inside for their own safety. Upon hearing their advice, Lizzie Borden asked if anyone in the household was suspected of committing the crime.

The mayor alluded to the mobbing of her uncle the night before. Lizzie Borden pressed on, asking whether she was suspected.

"Well, Miss Borden," he replied, "I regret to answer, but I must answer—yes, you are suspected."[36]

Telling Lizzie Borden she was a suspect was a mistake.[37] By admitting that Lizzie Borden was a suspect, the mayor unknowingly had set up a major obstacle for the prosecution. Lizzie Borden's statements at the upcoming questioning would later be ruled inadmissible as evidence.

chapter three

THE CASE BEGINS

FALL RIVER, MA—Fall River authorities were in a bind. As much as they suspected Lizzie Borden of murder, they had no solid proof. All they had was circumstantial evidence, details that seemed to point toward a conclusion, but were not absolute.

Lizzie Borden, by her own admission, was close in time and place to the murders. She also stood to inherit a great deal of money following the deaths of her father and stepmother. Her alibi, too, raised suspicions. When asked why she had gone to the barn, Lizzie Borden gave different answers to different people.

- To Dr. Bowen: She was looking for some iron or irons.

- To the mayor and a police officer: She was in the barn loft, eating some pears and looking for some lead to weigh down her fishing line.

- To Miss Russell: She was looking for a piece of iron or tin to fix a screen.[1]

Additional Suspicions

A search of the house showed *no* screen in need of

repair.[2] Lizzie Borden also raised suspicions by offering different versions about what she heard—or did not hear—just prior to discovering her father's body.

- To Officer Mullaly: She said she heard a peculiar noise, something like a scraping noise, and came in and found the door open.

- To Bridget Sullivan: She said she heard a groan and rushed in and found her father.

- To Officer Harrington: She said she did not hear any outcry or noise of any kind.[3]

Moreover, why would anyone spend twenty or perhaps thirty minutes in a stiflingly hot barn loft on an errand that should have taken only a few minutes? And why had no one come forward with information about the note summoning Abby Borden to visit a sick friend?

Convinced that Lizzie Borden had sole opportunity to commit the crime, police marshal Rufus B. Hilliard went to see the judge. On Monday morning, August 8, 1892, the marshal came away with a warrant for Lizzie Borden's arrest.

District Attorney Hosea Knowlton, though, persuaded him to keep the warrant in his pocket. To convict such a prominent young woman, the district attorney wanted some kind of proof to back up his case. He decided to call for an inquest, a legal procedure used to gather information. The inquest dates back to the seventeenth century, when judges in England traveled from village to village.[4] Authorities would call for a "coroner's jury" to investigate a violent or mysterious death that occurred between judicial sittings. Over the centuries, this form of investigation before a judge became known as an inquest.

The Inquest

District Attorney Knowlton took advantage of the inquest because it offered him more freedom than other legal proceedings. Because the inquest was not an accusatory procedure, witnesses did not have the right to be represented by lawyers. Prosecutors could therefore question witnesses more freely. The inquest was scheduled for August 9–11 before the judge, an old friend of Andrew Borden's.

Lizzie Borden's attorney, Andrew Jennings, asked for special permission to represent his client but was refused. Lizzie Borden agreed to testify on her own at the inquest. Had she refused to testify, she would have damaged her image as an innocent bystander.[5]

Supporters, meanwhile, rushed to Lizzie Borden's side. On Sunday, August 7, 1892, the congregation of the Central Congregational Church held a joint service with the First Church of Fall River. Paritioners packed the hall. The reverend pleaded for support of Lizzie Borden. "Let us ourselves curb our tongues and preserve a blameless life from undeserved suspicions," he said.[6]

Although Lizzie Borden was a grown woman of thirty-two, her supporters defended her as a "poor defenseless girl."[7] Many citizens blamed her woes on the supposed insensitivity of the Fall River Police Department. Angry letters denouncing the police poured into newspaper offices.

An editorial in Springfield's *Daily Republican* accused the police of incompetence, saying,

> Because someone, unknown to them and too smart for them to catch, butchered two people in the daytime on a principal street of the city, using brute force, far in excess of that possessed by this girl, they conclude that there is probable reason to believe that she is the murderess.[8]

The huge crowds outside the Borden house on Second Street blocked off carriage traffic during the day. When word of the inquest went out, curious onlookers rushed from Second Street to Court Square.

Newspaper articles reported that Bridget Sullivan was "deeply distressed" and broke frequently into sobs at the prospect of testifying at the inquest.[9] Other witnesses called and quizzed included pharmacist Eli Bence, Dr. Bowen, neighbor Adelaide Churchill, relative Hiram Harrington, as well as Lizzie Borden. Never again would Lizzie Borden take the stand in her own behalf.

The inquest was a secret proceeding that did not allow newspaper reporters. Accounts of the testimony came out later in the June 12, 1893, issue of *The Evening Standard* of New Bedford. The inquest began with Bridget Sullivan testifying about her whereabouts on the day of the murders. She revealed nothing she had not already told the police.

Lizzie Borden testified next. On all three days of the inquest, she gave snappish and confused answers, repeatedly contradicting herself. The morphine the doctor had prescribed to ease her nerves may have contributed to her confusion.[10]

On the first day of the inquest, Tuesday, August 9, 1892, the district attorney questioned Lizzie Borden about her father's financial situation. The district attorney wanted to show greed as the motive of the murders. Perhaps Lizzie Borden feared that her father was planning to leave his considerable estate to his wife instead of his daughters.

Q: Have you any idea how much your father was worth?

A: No sir.[11]

The district attorney moved on to her father's real estate holdings, then asked if she knew whether or not Andrew Borden had made a will.

The huge crowds that often gathered outside the Borden house on Second Street blocked off carriage traffic.

A: No sir, except I heard somebody say once that there was one several years ago; that is all I ever heard.

Q: Who did you hear say so?

A: I think it was Mr. Morse.[12]

By linking her uncle, John Vinnicum Morse, to her father's financial affairs, Lizzie Borden raised questions about Morse's visit. Was his appearance the day before the murders a mere coincidence? Or was it a factor to be considered in the murders?[13]

Next came the subject of Andrew Borden's supposed enemies. Once again, Lizzie Borden told the story about how her father had turned down a man's request for space to rent. She did not remember exactly when the argument had occurred but thought it was within the past couple weeks.

Q: Beside that, do you know of anybody that your father had bad feelings toward, or who had had feelings toward your father?

A: I know of one man who has not been friendly with him; they have not been friendly for years.

Q: Who?

A: Mr. Hiram C. Harrington.[14]

Lizzie Borden thus got even with the uncle who had spoken so negatively about her the day after the murders. Harrington was the husband of Andrew Borden's sister, Laurana. Lizzie Borden had a chilly relationship with Harrington, much as she did with her other uncle, John Vinnicum Morse. District Attorney Knowlton expressed only passing interest before turning his attention to the relationship between Lizzie Borden and her stepmother.

Relationship with Stepmother

The stepdaughter admitted to having had "words" with her stepmother over the Whitehead house but described it as a simple difference of opinion. The district attorney asked if she had been on pleasant terms with her stepmother since then. Lizzie Borden answered that she had. The district attorney pressed on.

Q: Cordial?

A: It depends upon one's idea of cordiality, perhaps.

Q: According to your idea of cordiality?

A: Quite so.[15]

The district attorney followed up by asking whether her relationship with her stepmother was that of daughter and mother.

A: In some ways it was, and in some it was not.

Q: In what ways was it?

A: I decline to answer.

Q: Why?

A: Because I do not know how to answer it.[16]

Lizzie Borden was more clear on how the relationship was *not* like that of daughter and mother. She did not call Abby Borden "mother." When she needed something, she turned to her older sister, Emma, rather than to her stepmother.

The district attorney asked Lizzie Borden whether her father and stepmother seemed happily married. She said they did. Then he turned to the question of her clothing.

Q: What dress did you wear the day they were killed?

A: I had on a navy blue silk skirt, with a navy blue blouse. In the afternoon, I put on a pink wrapper.[17]

Next, Lizzie Borden was asked about her whereabouts on the morning of the murders. At first, she said she was in the kitchen reading an old *Harper's* magazine when her father came home. Next she said she might have been in the dining room. Then she changed her story again and said she was on her way downstairs when he came home. She had taken up the clean clothes and had stopped to baste a piece of tape on a garment. Knowlton was confused. Hadn't she said she was downstairs—not upstairs—when her father returned home? Lizzie Borden made no attempt to hide her own confusion.

"I don't know what I have said," she began. "I have answered so many questions and I am so confused I don't know one thing from another. I am telling you just as nearly as I know how."[18]

She said she thought her stepmother was out visiting a sick friend on the morning of the murders. When pressed, she said she had not heard her leave. No, she did not hear her return. No, she did not tell Bridget Sullivan she thought her stepmother had returned home. Bridget Sullivan testified to the contrary.

On the second day of the inquest, the district attorney spent an hour quizzing Lizzie Borden about fishing lines and sinkers. She said she went to the barn loft to look for lead to use as weights on her fishing line. Why, the district attorney wondered, had she taken so long?

Heated Questioning

"I do not do things in a hurry," Lizzie Borden replied.[19]

Lizzie Borden was asked if she had done anything else while she was in the loft. Remembering her previous complaints of nausea, the district attorney asked how she was feeling compared to earlier that morning when she could not eat any breakfast.

A: I never eat any breakfast.

Q: You did not answer my question and you will, if I have to put it all day.[20]

The district attorney had lost his temper, which was a big mistake. He would later have trouble maintaining that Lizzie Borden had testified voluntarily at the inquest.[21]

Lizzie Borden insisted she felt well enough to eat the pears. She was then questioned about her resting place in the barn loft.

Q: I ask you why you should select that place, which was the only place which would put you out of sight of the house, to eat those three pears in?

A: I cannot tell you any reason.

Q: You observe that fact, do you not? You have put yourself in the only place perhaps, where it would be impossible for you to see a person going into the house?[22]

The district attorney returned to the events of earlier that morning. Lizzie Borden mentioned the sick note once again but also remembered asking her stepmother about her clothing. "I said to her, 'Won't you change your dress before you go out?' She had on an old one. She said, 'No, this is good enough.'"[23]

The prosecutor then asked about axes and hatchets. She said she knew of only one—an axe. Police remembered her telling them on the day of the murders about both a hatchet and an axe.

The judge asked if Lizzie Borden had made any effort to contact her stepmother upon discovering her father's body?

No, she replied; she thought Abby Borden was out on her sick call.

On the third day of the inquest, the district attorney asked Lizzie Borden about prussic acid. She denied not only trying to buy the poison but also visiting Smith's drugstore on Wednesday morning.

Q: Do you know where the drugstore is?

A: I don't.[24]

The drugstore was located on a main intersection only a few minutes from the home where Lizzie Borden had lived for the past fourteen years. The district attorney, however, dropped the subject.

In the course of questioning, Lizzie Borden contradicted

not only herself but also other witnesses. Bridget Sullivan said Lizzie Borden was upstairs when her father returned. Lizzie Borden agreed at first, then changed her mind and said she was in either the kitchen or somewhere else downstairs. She said her father had returned home at ten in the morning when, in fact, he was still downtown.[25]

When the inquest ended on Thursday, August 11, 1892, one week after the murders, the judge signed a warrant for Lizzie Borden's arrest.

The Arrest

The district attorney and the police marshal notified attorney Andrew Jennings of his client's upcoming arrest. With her lawyer by her side, Lizzie Borden received the warrant for her arrest. Because Fall River lacked facilities for female prisoners, she would stay in the matron's quarters. The arraignment, the proceedings at which she would plead either guilty or innocent, was scheduled for the following morning.

News of Lizzie Borden's arrest flashed around the world. Fall River's *Daily Globe* newspaper declared, "Locked Up: Lizzie Borden At Last In Custody."[26]

Emma Borden brought her sister a small suitcase of fresh clothes. The reverend came to visit. At 9:45 A.M. Lizzie Borden entered the courtroom for her arraignment, in which she would enter a formal plea to a charge. Asked how she pleaded, she said, "Not guilty."

Unsure of what he had heard, the clerk repeated his question.

"Not guilty," Lizzie Borden replied in a louder voice, accentuating the first word of her answer.[27]

Bail, the system allowing for the temporary release of a prisoner awaiting trial in exchange for money, did not exist in 1892 for people charged with murder. Judge Blaisdell ordered that Lizzie Borden be brought to the county jail in Taunton. It had facilities for female inmates.

Transporting the Prisoner

People outside the courtroom waited for a glimpse of the carriage taking Lizzie Borden to the railroad station. Crowds lined the main streets from the courthouse to the railroad station. But most people were disappointed. The carriage avoided the crowds by winding its way through the side streets. Crowds waited at the railroad platform in Taunton to catch a glimpse of the famous prisoner. Lizzie Borden arrived at the Taunton jail, where she received such special privileges as being taken out for walks.[28]

The legal road ahead would take Lizzie Borden on a ten-month journey from lower to higher courts. Because murder is such a serious crime, the state would need to prove "probable cause," reasonable grounds for believing that a person on trial is guilty of the crime charged, for the case to go forward from preliminary hearing to the grand jury. The grand jury is a judicial body that examines the evidence against the suspect to determine whether the case should be dismissed or tried before a judge and/or jury. If the grand jury decides that the case is valid, it issues an indictment, a formal criminal charge, against the suspect. Lizzie Borden ultimately would be tried before an all-male jury and a panel of three male judges, in keeping with the legal procedures of that time.

Lizzie Borden returned to Fall River for the preliminary hearing to be held August 22–28, 1892.

Preliminary Hearing

The pharmacist testified at the preliminary hearing that a woman had come into his store asking for prussic acid. Asked how he had identified her as Lizzie Borden, Eli Bence replied that the police had brought him to her house so he could identify her by her voice.

Defense attorney Jennings then asked if there was anything peculiar about Lizzie Borden's voice.

The pharmacist replied that it was unsteady, trembling.

Another witness, however, remembered the woman who had asked for prussic acid as speaking in a loud, steady voice.[29]

Lizzie Borden's inquest testimony was read aloud for the record. The long and rambling testimony, however, was hard to turn into a readable news story.[30] At the end of the hearing, the judge ruled that there was enough evidence for the case to go forward.

"Suppose," said the judge "that a *man* had been found in the vicinity of Mr. Borden and the only account he could give of himself was the unreasonable one that he was out in the barn looking for sinkers, that he was in the yard, that he was looking for something else," the judge said. "Would there be any question in the minds of men what should be done with such a man?"[31]

Tests of the axes and hatchets, meanwhile, came back showing no traces of blood. The stains were from rust; the gray hairs, from a cow.[32]

Newspaper reporters from around the world rushed to interview Lizzie Borden. The prisoner agreed to meet with only one—Kate Swan McGurk, an acquaintance from her days with the Fall River Fruit and Flower Mission. The article appeared in *The New York Recorder* on September 20, 1892.

"There is one thing that hurts me very much," Lizzie Borden said in the interview. "They say I don't show any grief. Certainly I don't in public. . . . They should see me when I am alone, or sometimes with my friends."[33]

The Grand Jury and the Dress Burning

The grand jury took up the case on November 15 but stopped deliberating temporarily on November 21, 1892, without making a decision. Lizzie Borden's friend Alice Russell, meanwhile, wrestled with her conscience.[34] Should she remain loyal to her friend? Or should she tell authorities what she knew about Lizzie Borden's suspicious behavior on the Sunday following the murders? She met with the district attorney and agreed to testify against Lizzie Borden.

The district attorney called the grand jury back into session. On December 1, 1892, Russell testified that she saw Lizzie Borden burn a dress. Russell told the grand jury that, on the Sunday morning after the murders, she entered the

Bordens' kitchen and found Lizzie Borden, in her sister's presence, ripping up a dress to burn in the stove.

"I am going to burn this old thing up," Lizzie Borden told Russell. "It is covered with paint."

Noticing the police outside, Russell warned her friend that someone might see her through the window. Lizzie Borden took a step back, then continued burning the dress. Russell left the house, then, upon being questioned by the police, returned the following day.

"I am afraid, Lizzie, the worst thing you could have done was to burn that dress," she said. "I have been asked about your dresses." To which Borden replied, "Oh, what made you let me do it?"[35]

After deliberating for ten minutes, the grand jury voted

to indict Lizzie Borden for murder. The same grand jury indicted Henry Trickey, the aptly named reporter for *The Boston Globe*, for tampering with witnesses. Trickey, though, could not be found. A few days later, the *Globe* announced, "Henry G. Trickey Dead: Although Only 24 Years Old, His Life Was Most Eventful."[36]

Because of Lizzie Borden's evasive answers, District Attorney Hosea Knowlton (shown here) lost his temper at the inquest.

Trickey reportedly was trying to board a train in Ontario, Canada, when he stumbled and fell under it.

Public support for Lizzie Borden, meanwhile, remained strong. Newspapers editorialized about her innocence. Women's groups passed resolutions of support. The Fall River Woman's Union passed a resolution declaring its faith in Lizzie Borden as a "sister tenderly beloved."[37]

District Attorney Hosea Knowlton doubted he could win his case against such a prominent young woman.[38] A graduate of Harvard Law School, the district attorney had served as a state representative and senator before becoming district attorney. He made it clear that he did not enjoy prosecuting Lizzie Borden. He repeatedly spoke about the task as his "painful duty."[39]

Insanity Plea

Finally, the district attorney came up with an idea for disposing of the case. If Lizzie Borden's attorney would agree to an insanity plea, the case would never have to come to trial. Knowlton turned to Marshal Hilliard for help. Police officers interviewed people throughout the city to see if anyone thought Lizzie Borden was insane. They reported back that many people thought the Bordens were peculiar, but that none was insane.[40]

The attorney general, meanwhile, consulted with Boston-area psychiatrists to get their input on the case. None found evidence of insanity. Nonetheless, the prosecutors invited attorney Andrew Jennings to the attorney general's office in Boston to see if he could be talked into a sanity examination for his client.

Andrew Jennings, however, wanted nothing that might call into question Lizzie Borden's alleged innocence.[41] He refused the request. With his plans wiped out, the district attorney began preparing for trial.

A few months before the trial, the district attorney received more disappointing news. The attorney general was bowing out of the trial due to his poor health. There may have been other reasons as well. "No lawyer who could have his choice would care to try a woman for her life," commented Fall River's *Daily Globe*.[42]

Since the state's top prosecutor—the attorney general— usually dealt with high-profile murder cases, his withdrawal was a severe blow for the prosecution's case.[43]

"Personally, I would like very much to get rid of the trial of the case and fear that my own feelings in that direction may have influenced my better judgment," the district attorney wrote to the attorney general in a letter dated April 24, 1893. "I feel this all the more upon your not unexpected announcement that the burden of the trial would come upon me."[44]

Lizzie Borden was charged with first-degree murder due to the severity of the crime. Second-degree murder applied to less serious crimes. In Massachusetts in 1892, first-degree murder carried the death penalty.

Prospective jurors in the case were asked if they objected to the death penalty. Those who did were excused. Out of the 108 possible jurors questioned, thirty-one were excused because they already had formed opinions about Lizzie Borden's guilt or innocence, sixteen because they held opinions against the death penalty, one because he was related to the defendant, and the rest because of advanced age.[45] Of the twelve jurors chosen, many had daughters who were about the same age as Lizzie Borden. Juries in 1892 were all male, so no women were included.

Women's rights supporters, including Lucy Stone, campaigned for women jurors, but they were unsuccessful.[46] Because the Lizzie Borden trial involved murder, a panel of three judges was required.

Another Murder

Shortly before the trial, another crime grabbed headlines, offering new hope for Lizzie Borden's supporters. On May 31, 1893, just five days before the start of the Lizzie Borden trial, twenty-two-year-old Bertha Manchester was killed in her Fall River home. The similarities to the Borden murders were uncanny. Bertha Manchester, too, was killed in broad daylight with a hatchet or an axe. On June 1, 1893, the headlines of *The Boston Globe* declared, "Startling Parallelisms—Many Points of Resemblance Found Between Borden and Manchester Murders."[47]

Because the two murders seemed like the work of the same person, Lizzie Borden benefited as a result. She was in custody at the time of the Manchester murder, and could not possibly have committed it. "Well," her attorney Andrew Jennings quipped, "are they going to claim that Lizzie Borden did this too?"[48]

On the day before the Borden trial got underway, the police arrested a disgruntled farm laborer for the murder of Bertha Manchester. By the time stories about the arrest hit the press, jurors in the Lizzie Borden case already had been ordered not to read the newspaper. They did not learn until later that the suspect in the Manchester case could not possibly have killed the Bordens as well. Jose Carreira had not arrived in the United States from his native country until April 1893—eight months after the Borden murders.

Whether the Manchester killing was a so-called "copycat" murder, patterned after the Borden slayings, no one could say for sure. Whatever the case, the timing could not have been better for Lizzie Borden.[49]

chapter four

THE CASE AGAINST LIZZIE BORDEN

COURT HOUSE—So far, the prosecution still had no clear murder weapon. Thinking it must be one of the two axes or two hatchets found in the Bordens' cellar, District Attorney Knowlton finally settled on the hatchet without its handle. It was covered with fine ashes, not dust like the other items in the basement.

Knowlton carried the case forward with William Moody, a district attorney from eastern Massachusetts, as his assistant. As a team, Knowlton and Moody were a study in contrasts.[1] The burly, round-headed Knowlton sometimes roared at his witnesses. The younger, trimmer Moody spoke in a calm, level voice. Knowlton and Moody faced a formidable defense team in which family lawyer Andrew Jennings took a back seat to George Robinson, the former governor of Massachusetts.

Opening Arguments

The trial opened on June 5, 1893. In his opening argument, Moody outlined the Commonwealth's three-part case against Lizzie Borden.[2]

- First, Lizzie Borden was predisposed to commit the crime. The prosecution would show that she had the motive or state of mind to have committed the murders. Moody spoke of the ill will that had developed between Lizzie Borden and her stepmother, saying, "There was built up between them by locks and bolts and bars, almost an impossible wall."[3]

- Second, Lizzie Borden did, in fact, commit the crimes. She had both the opportunity and the means to carry them out. The state pointed to the hatchet without a handle as the probable murder weapon. It looked like it had been washed and thrust to dry in a pile of ashes. Lizzie Borden might have disposed of the handle to get rid of evidence. By her own admission, she was in the house at the time of her stepmother's murder. She must have either heard the thud of the body crashing to the floor or seen the body itself.

- Third, Lizzie Borden's pattern of lies, inconsistent statements, and unusual acts showed a consciousness of guilt. The state maintained that Lizzie Borden had made up the story about her stepmother's sick call. "That statement," it declared, "we put forward as a lie; it was intended for no purpose except to stifle inquiry into the whereabouts of Mrs. Borden."[4]

In the days ahead, the state brought in witnesses to back up its points. The first witness, civil engineer Thomas Kieran, unwittingly scored points for the other side, however. After providing routine measurements—that the ceilings on the first floor measured six inches higher than the ceilings on the second floor, for example—Kieran mentioned an experiment he had performed to see whether the closet in the Bordens' front entryway was large enough to conceal a person (such as a murderer). It was.

Engineer's Experiment

On cross-examination, Jennings asked Kieran if he had performed any other experiments. The engineer answered yes, that he had asked his assistant to lie down on the floor in the guest bedroom in the same position as Abby Borden's body had been found. Then Kieran went up the stairs to see if he could see the body. At only one point on the stairway could he see his assistant. Even then, he said, it was only because he knew his assistant was there. At all other points it was virtually impossible to see him.

Court spectators murmured in excitement. The state's argument that Lizzie Borden should have seen her stepmother's body was being contradicted by one of its own witnesses. The chief justice pounded his gavel for order.

Jennings continued to cross-examine Kieran.

Q: How was it when you stood upon the floor of the hall upstairs, in front of the door which we will call Miss Lizzie's room?

A: I couldn't see him.

Q: As you stood in the hall did you stand in the hall in front of Miss Lizzie's room and look for him?

A: I did.

Q: Could you see any portion of his body from that position?

A: No sir.[5]

The prosecution had somewhat better luck with its next group of witnesses. Dressmaker Hannah Gifford, in particular, backed up the prosecutor's view of ill will between Lizzie Borden and her stepmother. The dressmaker said that Lizzie Borden had scolded her for calling the stepmother "Mother," objecting that she was a "good-for-nothing thing."

Dressmaker Gifford testified: "I said, 'Oh, Lizzie, you don't mean that?' And she said: 'Yes, I don't have much to do with her; I stay in my room most of the time.' And I said: 'You come down to your meals, don't you?' And she said: 'Yes, but we don't eat with them if we can help it.'"[6]

Bridget Sullivan detailed the menu at the Borden household on the morning of the murders, as follows: mutton, mutton broth, johnnycakes, coffee, cookies and butter, bananas, and other fruit. When she told of the heavy summer breakfast, she laughed. One newspaper reporter found it peculiar that a man as wealthy as Andrew Borden would feed his family leftover mutton.[7] After all, he could have afforded a higher-grade cut of meat.

Intruder not Likely

The prosecution set out to prove its second point by showing how unlikely it was for an intruder to have committed the crime. For someone to come through the house, hide, vanish, and leave no sign of break-in, all the while taking into account the delicate timing needed to commit the murders, defied the imagination. Who but an insider would know when Abby Borden would be alone in the guest room, Bridget Sullivan would be outside washing windows, Andrew Borden would be back from downtown, and John V. Morse would still be out of the house?[8]

Repairmen working in the neighborhood testified that they had seen no one entering or leaving the Bordens' house that morning. If Lizzie Borden were in the barn loft at the time of Andrew Borden's death, as she claimed, why had police Inspector William H. Medley found no footprints there? Medley testified to the extreme heat of the hayloft, adding support to the theory that Lizzie Borden had lied about her alibi.

The prosecution set out to show that the light blue figured dress was the robe of homicide. Adelaide Churchill scored a major point for the prosecution by testifying that, on the morning of the murders, she saw Lizzie Borden wearing a light blue calico dress decorated with a darker blue diamond pattern on it. When shown the dark blue two-piece silk dress Lizzie

Lizzie Borden's friend Alice Russell (shown here) was faced with a tough dilemma. She had to decide whether to remain loyal to her friend or testify for the prosecution. She eventually told the authorities about Borden's suspicious behavior on the Sunday following the murders.

Borden had surrendered to authorities, Mrs. Churchill was adamant that it was not the dress she was wearing on the morning of the murders.

Dr. Bowen's memory was more fuzzy. He could only describe the dress Lizzie Borden was wearing that fateful Thursday in August as "drab." He helped the prosecution, however, by saying that he would not describe the darker blue silk dress as drab.

Once again, Alice Russell testified about seeing Lizzie Borden burn a light blue figured dress.

> **Q:** (by Moody): Miss Russell, will you tell us what kind of a dress—give us a description of the dress she burned, that you have testified about, on Sunday morning.
>
> **A:** It was a cheap cotton Bedford cord.
>
> **Q:** What was its color?
>
> **A:** Light blue ground with a dark figure—small figure.[9]

The prosecution also questioned Miss Russell about her visit with Lizzie Borden on the night before the murder. It wanted to show that Lizzie Borden's stories about robberies and threats against her father were an attempt to turn suspicion away from herself before the crimes had been committed.[10]

The Hatchet Without a Handle

The prosecution then went on to argue that Lizzie Borden had the "means" to commit the crime with the hatchet that had no handle. The murderer, he said, had tried to hide evidence of the handle by burning it.

Detective Fleet testified about finding this hatchet without a handle in a box in the cellar. The handle was freshly broken off near the head of the hatchet. Unlike other items in the cellar, the hatchet head was covered with white ashes on both sides.

Fleet's cool, detailed testimony scored points for the prosecution. Impressed by Fall River's deputy marshal, *The New York Times* wrote, "Mr. Fleet's description of the weapon is so minute and his reputation for veracity is so great that belief in general is that he found the weapon with which the murder was committed."[11]

Next, the prosecution brought in medical experts to show that Lizzie Borden could have been the one who had committed the crimes with the hatchet. Lizzie Borden's supporters had maintained that, since no one had seen blood on her on the morning of the murders, someone else must have committed the crime. Dr. William A. Dolan, the Fall River medical examiner, argued that if the blows were delivered from a certain direction, the assailant would have remained clean. Dr. Dolan also argued that only moderate force was needed to deliver the blows. A woman of ordinary strength could have committed the murders.

Dr. Edward S. Wood, a professor of chemistry at Harvard Medical School, testified for the prosecution about the ashes on the hatchet without a handle. From the pattern of ashes on the hatchet head, he concluded that the hatchet had been forcibly rubbed with ashes. The handle, he believed, had been broken off after the murders. Dr. Wood also mentioned a small drop of blood found on Lizzie Borden's undergarments.

Although the defense attributed this small stain to menstrual blood, Dr. Wood testified that it had come from the outside, not the inside, of the garment. The prosecution, though, did not press its case. Perhaps the subject seemed too delicate.[12] Victorians rarely talked about women's bodily functions.

Next to take the stand was Boston physician Frank W. Draper, medical examiner for Suffolk County. In one of the most spectacular moments of the trial, Dr. Draper fitted the hatchet into the wounds of Andrew Borden's skull, which had been preserved as evidence. The 2.5-inch hatchet fitted the wounds exactly. The prosecution went on to make its point.

Q: Are you able to say whether or not this weapon could be capable of making these wounds?

A: I believe it is.[13]

Q: In your opinion, Dr. Draper, could the results you found have been produced by the strength of an ordinary hatchet, in the hands of a woman of ordinary strength?

A: They could, yes, sir.[14]

Cross-examination of Dr. Draper by the defense attorney, Melvin Adams, helped the prosecution's case. When Adams handed Dr. Draper a different hatchet with a blade edge roughly the same size, it did not fit.

Behavior After the Murders

The prosecution's third argument—consciousness of guilt—focused on Lizzie Borden's behavior after the murders. The fact that she had burned her dress, in particular, raised suspicions.

Also suspicious was the argument that police matron Hannah Reagan supposedly heard between Emma and Lizzie Borden. Hannah Reagan said that on the morning of August 24, 1892, she overheard Lizzie saying, "You have given me away, Emma, but I don't care. I won't give in one inch." To which Emma replied, "O Lizzie! I didn't."[15]

Inconsistencies in Lizzie Borden's alibi, too, raised suspicions. In an attempt to show that Lizzie Borden was never in the barn on the morning of the murders, Knowlton questioned Phoebe Bowen, the doctor's wife, about Lizzie Borden's hands on the morning of the murders. Mrs. Bowen had said her hands were clean. Did they look like she had been handling objects in a dusty barn loft? Knowlton asked. Phoebe Bowen replied that they did not.[16]

Inquest Testimony

The prosecution then called Annie White, the stenographer (the person who took notes) from the inquest. The defense objected, arguing that the inquest testimony should be excluded because Lizzie Borden had not testified voluntarily. Because she was virtually under arrest at the time of the inquest, the defense claimed she had been denied her rights to due process under the law. Moreover, she was under the effects of morphine at the time.

Adelaide Churchill (shown here) helped the prosecution by testifying that the dress Lizzie Borden surrendered to the authorities was not the same dress she wore the morning of the murders.

The district attorney responded that the inquest had been held lawfully and so her testimony was admissible. He cited numerous cases in which the testimony of suspects was considered voluntary. Moody said that hardly a court term passed in which testimony similar to Lizzie Borden's was not admitted.[17]

Lizzie Borden's lawyers argued that the decisions of the past were irrelevant. "The shield of the State and the shield of the nation are her protection in this hour," declared George Robinson, the chief defense attorney for the trial.[18]

Moody responded by saying that Robinson's argument was magnificent, but not the law. Knowlton, to be sure, had built a solid case based on legal history. Furthermore, Lizzie Borden had been in constant contact with her attorney Andrew Jennings *before* the inquest. Surely he must have informed her of her rights.[19]

The judges, though, sided with Robinson. Lizzie Borden, they decided, *had* been virtually under arrest at the inquest. Her inquest testimony, with all its contradictions, was excluded.

The Pharmacist and Prussic Acid

Pharmacist Eli Bence was then called to the stand, prompting yet another judicial debate. Bence testified that prussic acid was *not* used for the purpose of cleaning sealskin capes or capes of any kind. Defense Attorney Robinson objected to Bence's testimony, arguing that an alleged attempt to buy poison bore no relevance to the murders in question.

Moody maintained that the state of mind of the defendant just prior to the murders was, indeed, relevant. Once again, he carefully cited existing laws to back up his claim. The judges conferred, then declared that the prosecution needed to find witnesses to back up the pharmacist's opinion. Otherwise, Eli Bence's entire testimony would be excluded.

That evening, the prosecutors canvassed New Bedford in search of experts to back up their case. By the following morning, they had the following three people: a pharmacist, a chemist, and a furrier. The pharmacist and chemist insisted that prussic acid's lethal fumes ruled it out as an exterminating agent. The furrier testified that sealskin was naturally immune to moths since insect eggs did not hatch in it.[20]

Defense Attorney Robinson shot back the following hypothetical question: If there should ever be moths in sealskin, would prussic acid kill them?

The furrier admitted it would. Prussic acid would kill almost anything.

Both sets of attorneys approached the bench. Finally the judges reached a decision. Eli Bence's testimony would be excluded.

During the recess that followed, prosecutors Moody and Knowlton retreated to a private room of the courthouse. All of the prosecution's most vital evidence had been rejected. Moody fumed that the judges were thoroughly biased on Lizzie Borden's behalf.[21]

Closing Arguments

Nevertheless, the prosecution went back to work. District Attorney Hosea Knowlton delivered the closing arguments, speaking in lofty, majestic prose. His speech, with its high moral tone, had a biblical ring to it.[22]

He cautioned the jurors to perform their duty as men—not as gallants.[23]

Although he acknowledged that Lizzie Borden was a Christian woman, he argued that neither gender nor social class was a protection against crime. Those things should not stop the jurors from finding Lizzie Borden guilty, if all of the evidence pointed to her as the murderer.

Comparing women to men, he said: "If they lack in strength and coarseness and vigor, they make up for it in cunning, in dispatch, in celerity [haste], in ferocity. . . ." He mentioned the class differences between Lizzie Borden and Bridget Sullivan and asked, "Is there one law for Bridget and another for Lizzie?"[24]

Yet, despite such claims to equality under the law, many people found it hard to believe that a "lady" like Lizzie Borden would kill her own father. Knowlton offered the jurors consolation by suggesting that, while Lizzie Borden had coldly planned to murder her stepmother, she had made no such preparations for her father. Knowlton theorized that Lizzie Borden committed the second murder on the spur of the moment upon realizing that her father would know who had killed his wife.

But, once the deed had been done, Knowlton believed that Lizzie Borden had tried to cover it up. This, he believed, pointed to consciousness of guilt. By burning the dress, she had tampered with evidence, which, in itself, was a crime.

He dismissed the theory that an intruder could have committed the crimes. Would an intruder have left the house with a hatchet or an axe? This pointed, again, to the hatchet without a handle as the murder weapon.

Knowlton also addressed the nagging question of circumstantial evidence. Although eyewitness accounts, too, can be unreliable, circumstantial evidence has come under particular fire. Knowlton tried to persuade skeptics that circumstantial evidence was, indeed, valid when it established a chain of events. Pointing to the Borden case, he exclaimed, "Talk about a chain of circumstances!"[25]

He used an example from literature to illustrate the validity of circumstantial evidence. In the story of *Robinson Crusoe*, a man thinks he is alone on an island, then finds a fresh footprint in the sand.

The district attorney argued,

> His heart beat fast, his knees shook beneath him, he fell to the ground in fright because Robinson Crusoe knew when he saw that circumstance that a man had been there that was not himself. It was circumstantial evidence. It was nothing but circumstantial evidence. But it satisfied him.[26]

He also compared circumstantial evidence to a current of water. Speaking of "chips" of refuse floating on the surface of a stream, he raised the possibility of one hundred going in one direction and another dozen or two moving the other way. Even though all the chips were not going the same way, no one would doubt the direction of the current, he said.

"But you would not have any doubt, you would not hesitate for a moment, Mr. Foreman, to say that you knew which way the current of that river was," he said, "and yet you have not put your hand in the water; you have only seen things from which you inferred it, and even the things themselves did not all go the same way."[27]

"You are merciful men," he said. "The wells of mercy, I hope, are not dried up in any of it. But this is not the time nor the place for the exercise of it!"[28]

chapter five

DEFENDING LIZZIE BORDEN

COURT HOUSE—George Robinson brought years of experience as a politician to his position as head of Lizzie Borden's defense team.

At fifty-nine, the former three-term governor of Massachusetts was a powerful public speaker whose style greatly contrasted with District Attorney Knowlton's approach. Instead of preaching to the jurors, Robinson simply talked to them.[1] In plain, folksy language, he argued that it was impossible for a woman like Lizzie Borden to have committed such a crime.

On the advice of her attorneys, Lizzie Borden wore black to court to show that she was still in mourning.[2] The courtroom was packed. By the time of the trial, Lizzie Borden had become a household name. Throughout the thirteen days of the trial, however, she never took the stand on her own behalf.

Lizzie Borden sat quietly through most of the trial, although she occasionally fainted or covered her face in her hands in response to graphic testimony.[3] Many supporters viewed her as a poor victim—a real-life romantic heroine. Reporter Julian Ralph of *The New York Sun* wrote about Andrew Jennings's opening arguments, "For an hour he championed her cause with an ancient knight's consideration for her sex and for herself."[4]

Presumed Innocent

In the United States legal system, defendants are presumed innocent until proven guilty. The prosecution needed to prove Lizzie Borden "guilty beyond a reasonable doubt." Proof beyond a reasonable doubt means proof to a moral certainty—not proof beyond all doubt. If the law required proof beyond all doubt, few criminals would ever be convicted.[5]

Lizzie Borden's attorneys made no attempt to present their own theory of the crime. They did not have to; their client was presumed innocent. The prosecution would have to prove she was guilty. Instead, the defense attorneys spent much of their time attacking the prosecution's case by discrediting its witnesses. First, Robinson questioned Bridget Sullivan about the supposed discord between Lizzie Borden and her stepmother. When Bridget Sullivan mentioned that the Borden daughters and parents ate separately, he read back her testimony from the inquest.

Q: Did she always eat at the same table with Mr. and Mrs. Borden? And your answer: Always did eat dinner and supper when she was in the house.

A: Yes, sir, she ate the meals when she was in the house.

Q: That is so, is it? They always ate together when she was in the house, except when she was out on an errand. Is that so?

A: Yes, sir, they always ate together in the same dining room.[6]

Bridget Sullivan was being evasive. It took Robinson well over an hour to get her to admit to her previous testimony.

Q: Always ate together in the dining room?

A: Yes, sir.[7]

Scoring a victory on that point, Robinson moved on to the question of whether the maid might have left the side door unlatched on the day of the murders. If she had left the screen door unlatched, an intruder might have been able to enter. The defense wanted to discredit the prosecution's theory of exclusive opportunity.

Q: All the time that you were washing windows, that door was unhooked, wasn't it?

A: Yes, sir.[8]

Robinson went on to drive home his point.

Q: Can you tell me any reason why a person could have walked into that door and you not seen him?

A: Why, of course, they could.[9]

Cross-examination of Bridget Sullivan had been similar to that of engineer Thomas Kieran—damaging to the prosecution's case. Julian Ralph of *The New York Sun* wrote, "Most fair-minded persons here are of the opinion that there

This picture of Lizzie Borden was taken in 1893. Borden wore black to court to show that she was still in mourning.

has been nothing brought forward that does not tend to prove the woman innocent quite as much as to suggest her guilty."[10]

Prescription for Tranquilizers

The defense also scored points in its cross-examination of Dr. Bowen. In questioning by defense attorney Melvin O. Adams, the doctor admitted to having prescribed tranquilizers that might have affected Lizzie Borden's testimony at the inquest.

> **Q:** Does not morphine, given in double doses to allay mental distress and nervous excitement, somewhat affect the memory and change and alter the view of things and give people hallucinations?
>
> **A:** Yes sir.[11]

Courtroom spectators murmured in excitement. The defense had made a point Robinson would later emphasize in his closing.

The defense also discredited the prosecution's theory that the dress Lizzie Borden was wearing at the time of the murders was the one Alice Russell would see her burn. In interviews, District Attorney Knowlton had touted Alice Russell as the state's star witness.[12] The prosecution, however, succeeded in weakening her story about the dress.

Russell had testified that, while she could identify which dress had been burned, she could not remember what Lizzie Borden was wearing on the morning of the murders. Under cross-examination by former Governor Robinson, she said she had seen the light blue cotton Bedford cord dress only twice: in the spring it was made and, in the summer, on the fateful day it was burned. This contradicted the prosecution's theory that Lizzie Borden was wearing the dress at the time of the murders.

> **Q:** To make it clear, between the time you saw it on Miss Lizzie Borden and had the talk about it in the spring, you did not see it again until the Sunday morning after the homicide?
>
> **A:** I never remember of ever seeing it, and I am quite sure I did not—that I never had.[13]

Adelaide Churchill, too, cast doubt on the prosecution's theory about the dress. Under cross-examination, Churchill maintained that Bridget Sullivan was wearing a light-colored calico dress on the morning of the murders. Bridget Sullivan, however, testified that she was wearing a dark indigo-blue dress. If Mrs. Churchill was wrong about Bridget Sullivan's dress, she might be wrong about Lizzie Borden's, too. Thus her testimony that Lizzie Borden was wearing a light blue patterned dress on the morning of the murders was weakened.

The doctor's wife added to the confusion about the dress. When asked what Lizzie Borden was wearing on the morning of the murders, she replied that it was the dark blue silk dress the defendant had surrendered to the police.

Police Blunders

Cross-examination of the police, too, was damaging to the prosecution. Moody's contention, made in his opening statement, that the murderer had burned the hatchet handle to hide evidence of the crime came into question.

Officer Mullaly took the prosecution by surprise by saying that a broken handle was in the box with the hatchet that had no handle. Officer Fleet had testified that he saw only a hatchet head—no handle. Mullaly, however, insisted that Fleet had taken the handle out of the box. The prosecution never again mentioned the possibility that the hatchet handle had been burned in the stove.[14]

Further questioning revealed more police mistakes. Fleet said at first that Lizzie Borden's closet was not searched. One officer admitted losing the list of clothes in the defendant's closet. No one knew for sure whether the light blue Bedford cord dress was in the house at the time of one of the searches.

The defense also scored points with the prosecution's medical experts. Dr. Edward Wood, of Harvard Medical School, had found no trace of poison in the bodies of Abby and Andrew Borden. District Attorney Knowlton had indicated

George Robinson, a former three-term governor of Massachusetts, was Lizzie Borden's lead attorney. He asked the jurors if Lizzie Borden looked like the kind of fiend capable of committing the murders.

that the illness of the two elder Bordens might have been due to a poison attempt.[15]

In his cross-examination of Dr. Wood, defense attorney Melvin Adams cast doubt on the hatchet without a handle as the probable murder weapon. When asked about how difficult it would be to remove blood from the hatchet, Dr. Wood mentioned places on the hatchet head where blood would have been difficult to remove. Dr. Wood also mentioned the presence of dirt. This contradicted the prosecution's theory that the hatchet had been freshly washed.[16]

Victories for the Defense

By the time the prosecution rested, Lizzie Borden's attorneys had scored numerous victories. And they had yet to call their own witnesses and deliver their own opening and closing arguments.

On the tenth day of the trial, Thursday, June 15, 1893, attorney Andrew Jennings delivered an emotional opening for the defense.

> You are not sitting here to answer the question how this deed could have been committed or even who committed it; that is not the issue at all. The Commonwealth here has charged that Lizzie Andrew Borden, in a certain way, at a certain time, killed with malice or forethought. And that, and that alone, is the question you are to answer.[17]

Jennings questioned the prosecution's dress-burning theory. He asked why, if the dress were an indication of guilt, would Lizzie Borden burn it in broad daylight with officers on every side of the house?[18]

The defense then produced witnesses to show that someone other than Lizzie Borden might have committed the murders. One witness testified about overhearing a man angrily conversing with Andrew Borden. Others had seen strange-looking men in the neighborhood on the day of or before the murders.

Hiram Lubinsky, an ice cream vendor, said that he had passed the Bordens' house on the morning of the murders and seen a woman walking from the barn toward the rear-screen door. He thus confirmed Lizzie Borden's alibi of being in the barn at the time of the murders. However, when pressed about the exact time of his visit, Lubinsky could not say.

Two boys, Everett Brown and Thomas Barlow, said they had been in the barn loft on the morning of the murders, thus calling into question Officer Medley's testimony about the lack of footprints. Once again, the prosecution raised doubts about the timing. Neither boy could pinpoint the exact time of their visit.

Alleged Quarrel

The next five witnesses called into question Hannah Reagan's testimony about the alleged quarrel between the Borden sisters. Thomas F. Hickey, a reporter for *The Boston Herald*, for instance, testified about what Matron Reagan had said about the alleged quarrel saying, "There is no truth at all in the story that was printed."[19]

In the afternoon of the eleventh day of the trial, the

defense produced its star witness—Emma Borden. Emma Borden came out strongly on her sister's side.

Jennings set out to establish that a desire for the inheritance was not the motive. Emma Borden produced records to show that her sister had close to three thousand dollars in the bank and various shares of stock. By 1892 standards, this was an extraordinary amount of money for a young woman to have.[20]

Next, Jennings asked Emma Borden about the relationship between her sister and her father. She indicated that they were close by speaking of the gold ring, a gift from her sister, that their father had worn constantly until his death.

Emma Borden then testified that she had urged her sister to destroy the blue cotton Bedford cord dress the day before it was burned. She had noticed her younger sister's dress hanging on a nail while looking for a place to hang her own clothes.

"'You've not destroyed that old dress yet,' I said to Lizzie. She said: 'I think I will,' and I said: 'I would if I were you.'"[21]

Emma Borden was adamant that Matron Reagan's story about the quarrel with her sister had no basis in fact. She spoke up firmly when questioned by Jennings.

Q: Now, Miss Emma, on that morning did you have any conversation with Miss Lizzie in which she said, "Emma, you have given me away, haven't you?"

A: I did not.

Q: And did you say in reply, "No, Lizzie, I haven't"?

"You have," she says, "and I will let you see I won't give in one inch." Was there any such talk as that?

A: There was not.

Q: Anything like it?

A: Nothing.

Q: That morning or any morning.

A: No time, not any time.[22]

In his cross-examination of Emma Borden, District Attorney Knowlton asked about the relationship between her younger sister and her stepmother. Knowlton focused on the conflict over the purchase of the house in Abby Borden's name. Emma Borden presented herself as the more difficult stepdaughter.

Q: Were the relations between you and Lizzie and your stepmother as cordial after that occurrence of the house that you have spoken of as they were before?

A: Between my sister and Mrs. Borden they were.

Q: They were entirely the same?

A: I think so.

Q: Were they so on your part?

A: I think not.[23]

Closing Arguments

On Monday, June 19, 1893, George Robinson delivered his closing arguments. Playing on the jury's natural reluctance to believe that a woman had committed such a crime, he spoke warmly of Lizzie Borden's "humanly feeling and womanly bearing."[24] He downplayed the fact that the hatchet with no handle fit the wounds perfectly by saying, "This is an Underhill hatchet made by the Underhill Manufacturing Company; thousands of these were made and sold—you and I remember them as boys."[25]

Throughout his four-hour speech, the former governor stressed the choice available to the jury: either sentence Lizzie Borden to death or set her free. It was not the jurors' business to unravel the mystery of the murders, he said. Instead, the jury needed to confine itself solely to the question of whether the accused could be found guilty beyond a reasonable doubt.

Dismissing the prosecution's entire case as circumstantial, Robinson declared,

> Now, there is absolutely no direct evidence against Miss Borden. Nobody saw or heard anything or experienced anything that connects her with the tragedy. No weapon whatever, and no knowledge of the use of one, as to her, has been shown.[26]

Robinson played up the nineteenth-century belief in the sanctity of the home. Whatever Andrew Borden's home lacked in fancy luxuries, he made up for in simple, country comforts. Mutton was an ordinary, country breakfast—not the kind of fare served in a hotel, but perhaps more hearty.[27] Lizzie Borden was home on the morning of the murders because, after all, it was her home.

"I don't know where I would want my daughter to be," said Robinson, "than to say that she was at home, attending

Emma Borden (shown here) strongly defended her sister. During her testimony, Emma Borden explained that her relationship with her stepmother soured after her father purchased a house in Abby Borden's name. She then claimed that the relationship between Lizzie and their stepmother did not worsen.

to the ordinary vocations of life, as a dutiful member of the household, as belonging there. So, I do not think there is any criminal look about that."[28]

Next, Robinson moved on to the question of the note that supposedly summoned Abby Borden to visit a sick friend. Why, he asked, had the messenger not come forward? Some people, he exclaimed, simply did not like to come to court. After bending the truth to claim that Abby Borden had told Bridget Sullivan about the note (the maid testified that she had heard about the note from the stepdaughter, not the stepmother), Robinson theorized that the note probably had been burned.[29]

Robinson shot down the prosecution's theory of hatred between Lizzie Borden and her stepmother. The bonds of motherhood were so strong, he said, it was natural for Lizzie Borden to be reluctant to embrace a newcomer after losing her own mother. Referring to Abby Borden as her "stepmother" did not make Lizzie Borden a criminal.

"Why Martha Chagnon, that was here a day or two ago, stepped on the stand and began to talk about Mrs. Chagnon as her stepmother. Well, I advised the City Marshal to put a cordon around *her* house, so that there will not be another murder there."[30]

Still, he admitted that harsh words could be a problem. Everyone should be patient and kind. It was wrong for Lizzie Borden to speak ill of her stepmother.

"I agree with you that Lizzie A. Borden is not a saint," he said, "and, saving your presence, I have some doubts whether all of you are saints; that is to say whether you really never speak hurriedly or impatiently."[31]

The former governor raised question after question to discredit the prosecution's case. If Lizzie Borden were the assailant, why would she vouch for the innocence of John Morse and Bridget Sullivan in her interview with Officer Fleet? Why, if she were the assailant, had she not sent the maid out on an errand? And, how could Lizzie Borden be the murderer, if there was not a trace of blood on her body?

He dismissed the prosecution's claim of sole opportunity by maintaining that an intruder could have gotten in through the side door between 9:00 and 11:00 that morning. Once again, he raised the issue of the death penalty. Robinson pleaded with the jurors to spare Lizzie Borden's life.

"In the old days," Robinson said, "they had sacrifices of lambs and goats, and even human beings were offered in . . . sacrifice. But we have gotten over all that. We do not even burn witches now. . . ."[32]

Then he made a folksy appeal to the jurors.

"To find [Lizzie Borden] guilty, you must believe she is a fiend. Gentlemen, does she look it?"[33]

chapter six

THE DECISION

VERDICT—On Tuesday, June 20, 1893, the final day of the trial, the presiding judge offered Lizzie Borden the chance to speak for herself.

The defendant rose slowly and said, "I am innocent. I leave it to my counsel to speak for me."[1]

Associate Justice Justin Dewey, one of the three judges in the case, addressed the jury. Judge Dewey had been appointed to the bench by George Robinson, the governor of Massachusetts at that time. Although judges were supposed to leave the weighing of evidence to the jurors, Judge Dewey took it on himself to guide them. As the father of three daughters, Judge Dewey clearly sympathized with Lizzie Borden.[2]

First, he spoke about Lizzie Borden's high moral character. Whether good character, in itself, could render a defendant not guilty was a matter of debate, nonetheless, the judge presented it as a solid point in Lizzie Borden's favor. "In some cases it may not be esteemed of much importance," he said about a defendant's character. "In other cases it may raise a

/

reasonable doubt of a defendant's guilt even in the face of strongly criminating circumstances."[3]

Judge Dewey also called into question the credibility of some of the prosecution's witnesses. Young women, he said, tended to exaggerate their likes and dislikes. The judge came down particularly hard on dressmaker Hannah Gifford. Her testimony, he said, needed to be evaluated with care since hers was "the language of a young woman and not of a philosopher or a jurist."[4]

He also urged the jurors to use caution when evaluating the medical testimony. Although the five medical witnesses generally agreed with one another, Judge Dewey hinted at conflicts among them by saying, "It is a matter of frequent observation to see experts of good standing expressing conflicting and irreconcilable views upon questions arising at a trial."[5] He also pointed to differences in opinion about what Lizzie Borden was wearing on the morning of the murders.

> Is there such an agreement among these witnesses to whom no wrong intention is imputed by anybody . . . that you could put their statements together, and from those statements say that any given dress was accurately described?[6]

Judge Dewey looked more kindly on inconsistencies in Lizzie Borden's own statements. Oral statements, he said, were often subject to misinterpretation. He maintained that Lizzie Borden's failure to testify on her own behalf should not be held against her.

Discounting the prosecution's theory that there was no note about a sick call by Abby Borden, Judge Dewey offered the possibility that an outside assassin had sent it, then committed the murders, and destroyed the evidence. He offered no explanation for why the imaginary killer would want to lure out the victim-in-waiting.

A Plea for the Innocent

Rarely had a judge come out so strongly in favor of the defendant. Judge Dewey's charge to the jury surprised even Lizzie Borden's strongest supporters. One headline declared, "Judge's Charge a Plea for the Innocent."[7]

The twelve jurors, meanwhile, filed into the jury room to consider their verdict. Instead of taking time to examine the materials before them, the jurors came to a quick decision on the first vote. But, to avoid the appearance of having made up their minds ahead of time, they stayed in the room and chatted for a while.[8]

After an hour and a half, the foreman rang his bell to signal the jury was ready. "What say you, Mr. Foreman. . ." the clerk began.

Before he could finish, the foreman cried out, "Not guilty!"[9]

Acquitted

A loud yell rang out through the courtroom. Lizzie Borden had been acquitted (found not guilty of the crime charged). Spectators cheered and waved their handkerchiefs. No one tried to impose order. Defense attorney Andrew Jennings cried out, "Thank God!"[10]

Lizzie Borden clutched the rail in front of her and

sobbed. Then, clinging to her sister Emma, she said, "I want to go home. Take me straight home tonight."

"Tonight?"

"Yes, tonight. I want to see the old place and settle down at once."[11]

It took an hour to clear the courtroom as well-wishers kept wanting to shake hands with Lizzie Borden.[12] Outside the courthouse, thousands of people jammed the streets, waiting to catch a glimpse of the newly freed woman. When she finally appeared, bound for her waiting carriage, crowds cheered. Lizzie Borden instructed her driver to wait so she could shake hands with everyone. Parents lifted babies for her to kiss.

People in Fall River, meanwhile, streamed into Second Street to welcome back the woman who had become so well known in the past ten months. A special squad of police was needed to maintain order. By ten that night, the crowds reached some two thousand people. A band stopped in front of the house and played "Auld Lang Syne."[13]

To avoid the crowds in front of her house, the carriage brought Lizzie Borden to the home of friends a few blocks away. She told reporters that she was "the happiest woman in the world."[14]

Newspapers across the country hailed the verdict. Headlines proclaimed, "A Day of Sunshine for Lizzie, Back in Her Old Home, Friends Warmly Welcome Lizzie Home," and "Church and Charity May Claim Her."[15]

The New York Times, too, praised the decision. An editorial on June 21, 1893, described the defendant as "the most

Emma Borden (right) and Lizzie Borden listen closely to detailed testimony at the trial.

unfortunate and cruelly persecuted woman." The *Times* laid much of the blame for her plight on the Fall River police:

> The police are of the usual inept and stupid and muddle-headed sort that such towns manage to get for themselves. There is nothing more merciless than the vanity of ignorant and untrained men charged with the detection of crime, in the face of a mystery that they cannot solve, and for the solution of which they feel themselves responsible.[16]

That same day, June 21, 1893, the Associated Press interviewed Defense Attorney George Robinson. The former governor said that he never once doubted his client's innocence. Asked what had given him such confidence, he replied, "Her appearance, and above all, her perfect fairness in considering others who were at first under suspicion . . . lest some innocent person should be wrongly accused."[17]

New Doubts

Before long, however, the public turned against Lizzie Borden. People everywhere began to ask: If Lizzie Borden did not murder her parents, *who* did? Hatchets and axes kept turning up, but none fit the crime. Marshal Rufus B. Hilliard marked the case "closed."

Newspaper headlines blared, "Perhaps Murderer or Murderess May Be in the City. Who Can Tell?"[18] Providence's *Journal* newspaper concluded that Lizzie Borden had had sole opportunity to commit the crime. In its lead editorial on June 21, 1893, the *Journal* declared, "There is no reason now for Miss Borden's silence."[19]

Legal experts, too, began to have doubts. Judge Charles

G. Davis maintained that, as a result of Judge Dewey's bias, the Commonwealth did not receive a fair trial.[20] Professor John H. Wigmore, of Northwestern University Law School, insisted that Lizzie Borden's failure to take the stand could, indeed be held against her.

"The statements about the purpose of the barn visit, and about the discovery of the father's death, are frightfully inconsistent; while the story of the note requires for its truth a combination of circumstances almost inconceivable," wrote Wigmore in the 1893 issue of the *American Law Review.*

> Why did the accused not take the stand to explain these things? Of course, it was her legal right to remain silent . . . [but] we can not help feeling that she failed to explain them because she could not; and one side of the balance sinks heavily.[21]

Although the jury freed her, public opinion began to convict her. Few people wanted to be seen with the accused murderer. The one time Lizzie Borden went back to church, parishioners in nearby pews moved away from her. She never returned.[22]

The Borden sisters bought a grand mansion on The Hill. Their new home, hemmed in by maple trees, had four real bathrooms—unlike the primitive one in the basement on Second Street. Lizzie Borden christened it Maplecroft.

Elegance reigned supreme at Maplecroft, complete with archways and gold-leaf trim. The third floor housed the servants' quarters. Lizzie Borden had two bedrooms—one for summer, the other for winter.

From Lizzie to Lizbeth

Lizzie Borden started calling herself by the more aristocratic-sounding Lizbeth. Although she did not change her name legally, she had calling cards for visitors made up in the name of Lizbeth. Few people called, however.

Behind her back, people snickered about how the new Lizbeth was a "self-made heiress."[23] Lizzie Borden's old supporters in the Women's Christian Temperance Union (W.C.T.U.) wanted nothing to do with her. She, in turn, evicted the W.C.T.U. from its quarters in the A. J. Borden building. Children everywhere skipped rope to the rhyme:

> *Lizzie Borden took an axe*
> *And gave her mother forty whacks;*
> *When she saw what she had done,*
> *She gave her father forty-one.*

The rhyme, however, contained several inaccuracies.[24] Lizzie Borden was acquitted of the crime of murdering her father and *step*mother (not her mother). Authorities attributed the murders specifically to a hatchet, rather than an axe, and the actual number of blows was much lower than forty and forty-one respectively. There were nineteen blows for Abby Borden and eleven blows for Andrew Borden.[25]

Lizzie Borden stayed in Fall River because, she said, "when the truth comes out about the murder, I want to be living here. . . ."[26] She developed a passion for the theater, despite the disapproval of her older sister. Lizzie Borden traveled to shows in Boston and New York.

Back in Fall River, people pointed and stared whenever

they saw Lizzie Borden. She stopped going out to stores. Newspaper reporters camped in front of her house, but she refused to see them. Newspapers printed rumors as facts.

In 1894, Edwin Porter, a reporter for Fall River's *Daily Globe*, published a book about the Borden murders called *The Fall River Tragedy*. Porter's book made a strong case for the defendant's guilt. Rumors circulated that Lizzie Borden bought up most copies of the book and had them burned. Whatever the case, *The Fall River Tragedy* became a rare book.[27]

In December 1896, when Lizzie Borden was thirty-six years old, newspapers carried stories that she was engaged to be married. No reporter, however, was able to interview Lizzie Borden for the story. Whether the articles had any basis in fact remains a mystery. The alleged groom-to-be, a Swansea, Massachusetts, schoolteacher, went into hiding. Lizzie Borden never married.

Two months later, in February 1897, Lizzie Borden was back in the news after the owners of a store in Providence, Rhode Island, accused her of shoplifting two paintings. A customer had come in to have one of the paintings fixed, saying she had received it as a gift from Lizzie Borden. The store, however, had no record of the sale. "Two Paintings Missed From Tilden-Thurber Co.'s Store," blared the headlines in the February 16, 1897, *Daily Journal*.[28] A warrant was issued for Lizzie Borden's arrest, but the matter was dropped after a settlement was reached out of court.[29] The warrant was never served.

Lizzie Borden befriended a free-spirited actress, Nance

O'Neil. Rumors circulated that Lizzie Borden was writing a play in which Nance O'Neil would star. Perhaps Nance O'Neil saw in Lizzie Borden a similarity to the tragic women she played on stage. Perhaps O'Neil felt sorry for Lizzie Borden.

"Someone has pointed out to me recently, that I have nearly always interpreted the unloved woman in the theatre, the woman crucified by the unseen, the conventional traditions," Nance O'Neil later wrote in a magazine article. "Often in women who live out their destinies in the small places into which they been driven, there is a storm that broods but never bursts."[30]

Rift Between Sisters

One night in 1905, Lizzie Borden threw a lavish party for Nance O'Neil and her entire troupe at Maplecroft, complete

When the jury (shown here) acquitted Lizzie Borden, the entire courtroom erupted in celebration. Spectators cheered and waved their handkerchiefs. The streets were packed with thousands of people who cheered when Borden appeared from the courthouse.

with caterers and an orchestra.[31] An enraged Emma Borden moved out, eventually settling in Newmarket, New Hampshire. The two sisters never spoke again.[32]

Lizzie Borden remained at Maplecroft. Although socially an outcast, she lived like the queen of her own little castle. She employed a housekeeper, a cook, a second maid, and a coachman (a driver for her horse-drawn carriage). She treated them well, earning their loyalty. On hot days, she brought out cold drinks for her workers and told them to leave early even though she paid them for their full hours.[33] Lizzie Borden also loved animals and could be seen scattering peanuts on the lawn for squirrels.

Other participants in the Borden saga continued to be known for their roles in the case. Defense Attorney George Robinson retired to his private practice in Chicopee, Massachusetts, after collecting a hefty twenty-five thousand dollars from his most famous client. He died in 1900. District Attorney William Moody went on to become attorney general of the United States and an associate justice of the Supreme Court.

Prosecutor Hosea Knowlton took over Arthur Pillsbury's job as attorney general. Shortly before his death in 1902, Knowlton said that, if he had known what Andrew Borden and John V. Morse talked about on the night before the murders, he could have convicted somebody of the murders.[34]

Bridget Sullivan reportedly told a friend that Lizzie Borden had paid for her to return to Ireland. The defendant's lawyer, she said, had advised her not to return to the United

States.[35] Bridget Sullivan bought a farm in Ireland for her parents but, upon becoming restless, decided to return to the United States. She settled in Butte, Montana, marrying a man whose last name was also Sullivan.

In 1913, twenty years after the trial, Emma Borden broke her twenty-year-long silence on the case. "Guilty— No! No!" the headlines declared.[36] Reaffirming her belief in her sister's innocence, Emma Borden pointed to Lizzie's affection for "dumb animals" as proof of her innocence. "She fairly dotes on the dogs, cats and squirrels that are at the French street mansion," Emma Borden said. "Now anyone with a heart like that could never have committed the awful act for which Lizzie was tried and of which she was acquitted."[37]

Emma Borden, however, admitted that her sister could be peculiar. "Queer? Yes, Lizzie is queer," Emma Borden said. "But as for her being guilty, I say 'No,' and decidedly 'No.'"[38] Emma Borden said she had made a pledge to her dying mother to always take care of baby Lizzie.[39]

Nance O'Neil, meanwhile, drifted out of Lizzie Borden's life. Lizzie Borden continued to travel and take in plays, however. She also quietly took part in charitable pursuits, donating books, caring for stray animals, and financing the college education of a few local students. Lizzie Borden's old horse-drawn carriage gave way to a motorcoach.

In 1919, Lizzie Borden's old colleagues in the Women's Christian Temperance Union scored a major victory when Prohibition passed, making alcoholic beverages illegal. The

Gilded Age gave way to the Jazz Age, also known as the Roaring Twenties. Women won the right to vote in 1920.

As far as anyone knew, Lizzie Borden never discussed the murders with anyone. A fellow animal lover, though, said Lizzie Borden had come to regret her decision to stay in Fall River. A few townspeople, however, became fond of the white-haired woman. She bought lemonade and raffle tickets from neighborhood children.

Like her father, Lizzie Borden had a shrewd business sense. In 1925, she bought out her sister's share of the A. J. Borden Building in downtown Fall River. As sole owner, she saw the property values increase. She could afford to live more extravagantly than her older sister—buying diamonds and sapphires.

Hospital Stay

In 1926, Lizzie Borden arrived at the hospital for a gall bladder operation. (The gall bladder is a small sac on the underside of the liver. It holds a fluid that helps the body digest fatty foods. It also rids the body of certain waste products.) Nurses later remembered her as a difficult patient who had her chauffeur bring in special food from a local caterer. Orange sherbet was her favorite.

Lizzie Borden never fully recovered from her operation. She died on June 1, 1927, after suffering from pneumonia. In her will, she explained that she had left nothing to her sister, Emma, as she had her own share of their father's estate. Lizzie Borden set aside five hundred dollars for the care of her father's burial plot. Although she left some money to cousins, servants, and friends, her largest single bequest—thirty thousand dollars—went to the Animal Rescue League of Fall River. "I have been fond of animals, and their need is great, and there are so few who care for them," she stated in her will.[40]

Lizzie Borden's coachman, chauffeur, and gardener carried her casket. She was buried in the family plot, next to her father. Emma Borden died only nine days later and was buried next to her sister.

chapter seven

THE CONTINUING FASCINATION

EFFECTS ON HISTORY— Since ancient times, people have expected children to love and honor their parents. This expectation is, in fact, one of the Ten Commandments. The very idea that children might murder their parents has horrified—and fascinated—people throughout history. If the taking of another life is drama, then the taking of a parent's life is high drama.

Of all the types of murder, killing one's parents is the rarest.[1] Even today, in this age of widespread violence, such murders are relatively rare.[2] A recent study in the United States found some three hundred murders of parents by children each year.[3] The number of parents killed during the Victorian era was undoubtedly much lower.

For a woman like Lizzie Borden to be accused of killing not just one, but both of her parents, was a most unusual occurrence in the annals of crime.[4] The wealth and respectability of the victims, too, made the crime all the more memorable. Had the victims not been so well known and wealthy, the murders undoubtedly would have attracted far less publicity and attention.[5]

The case also included a number of bizarre features that made it particularly memorable.[6] Among them: the poison to clean a cape, the mysterious note about a supposed sick friend of Abby Borden's, and Lizzie Borden's inability to account for her whereabouts at the time of the murders.

An Influential Author

In the 1920s and 1930s, true-crime writer Edmund Lester Pearson introduced a new generation of readers to the Lizzie Borden saga. In 1924, just as the Borden murders were fading from memory, Pearson published *Studies in Murder*, using his first chapter to outline the case. His continued fascination with the case led to subsequent articles and chapters in books, culminating in 1937 with *The Trial of Lizzie Borden*.

The Trial of Lizzie Borden, a day-by-day account of the trial, was damaging to Lizzie Borden as Pearson clearly believed that she had gotten away with murder.[7] A librarian by profession, Pearson was a scholar held in high regard by his colleagues. *The Trial of Lizzie Borden* quickly became a starting point for anyone writing about the Borden case.[8]

In 1948, Agnes DeMille produced her ballet, *Fall River Legend*, based on the Borden murders, although the family is never mentioned by name. Lizzie Borden is simply called the accused, and, unlike in real life, she is found guilty of the murders. The ballet opens with the accused approaching the gallows. Although DeMille took liberties with the facts, she reportedly captured the dark, brooding spirit of the case.[9]

"Lizzie's life," wrote DeMille, "consisted mainly in things . . . that didn't happen. And how does one put in action, lack of dynamics, the maintenance of status quo into dance? How does one express boredom on stage?"[10] She accomplished this through dance, pantomime, and stark sets, rather than spoken words.

The case also inspired an opera and several plays, including one for television. Nonfiction writers, meanwhile, churned out countless articles and books about the case. Some writers who believed that Lizzie Borden was guilty nevertheless found reason to sympathize with her.

Lizzie Borden as Victim

In the 1953 book, *The Girl in the House of Hate*, authors Charles and Louise Samuels portray Lizzie Borden as a victim of a society that regarded women as inferior to men. By their standards, she was a modern-day feminist. The authors who seemed shockingly willing to justify murder said, "If today's woman has come out of the kitchen, she is only following Lizzie, who came out of it with a bloody ax and helped start the rights-for-women bandwagon rolling."[11]

Author Edward Radin, too, sympathized with Lizzie Borden, but for different reasons. He believed that she was innocent. In *Lizzie Borden: The Untold Story*, his best-selling 1961 book, Radin theorized that Bridget Sullivan killed Abby and Andrew Borden.

Radin read the original trial transcripts and concluded that Edmund Pearson's account was biased because it left out material that was favorable to the defendant. Bridget Sullivan, he said, had ample opportunity to commit the crime.

But what was her motive? Radin raised the possibility that the maid resented being asked to clean the windows on such a hot day when she was not feeling well.[12]

Radin's book caused a stir. A careful researcher, he had

After the trial ended, the Borden sisters bought a mansion on The Hill in Fall River. Lizzie Borden called it Maplecroft. The mansion was extremely elegant, with archways and gold-leaf trim. Lizzie Borden had two bedrooms—one for the summer, the other for winter.

been the first since Pearson to go back to the original trial transcripts. The book was well received by authorities in the field of fact-crime writing.

Still, many people continued to believe that Lizzie Borden was guilty. Writer Dorothy Parker observed, "I will believe till eternity, or possibly beyond it, that Lizzie Borden did it with her little hatchet, and whoever says she didn't commits the sin of sins, the violation of an idol."[13]

More new theories followed. In 1967, author Victoria Lincoln maintained in *A Private Disgrace: Lizzie Borden By Daylight* that Lizzie Borden suffered from epilepsy, and that her seizures somehow contributed to the murders. John Vinnicum Morse's visit, too, had helped trigger the murders. Lincoln theorized that Lizzie Borden wanted money and freedom and so intended to kill her father and stepmother with poison. On the morning of the murders, however, an epileptic seizure prompted her to kill them with an axe.

Other theories held that yet someone else had committed the murders. Like Kennedy assassination buffs, the new Borden theorists spent years rearranging established facts and props in startling new patterns.[14] In 1984, author Frank Spiering concluded in *Lizzie* that Emma Borden had secretly returned from Fairhaven to murder her parents.

History professor Bruce Laurie of the University of Massachusetts at Amherst has not been impressed. Observed Laurie, "Most of it is done by people with axes to grind— literally."[15]

Hundredth Anniversary

The hundredth anniversary of the murders in 1992 brought a new flurry of interest in the case. David Kent, in collaboration with Robert Flynn, published *The Lizzie Borden Sourcebook*, a collection of newspaper clippings about the case. The book jacket declared that Lizzie Borden had become an American legend much like Johnny Appleseed or Billy the Kid.[16]

On August 3, 4, and 5, 1992, Bristol Community College in Massachusetts hosted a conference on Lizzie Borden titled "The Legend 100 Years After the Crime." Scholars delivered papers aimed at separating fact from myth. Even the simplest-seeming facts—the weather on the day of the murders, for example—were subject to debate.

In *The Borden Case: Myths vs. Facts*, William L. Masterson argued that a Fall River newspaper set the maximum temperature for the day at 72 degrees.[17] The sweltering heat described by so many writers was a myth. Fall River Historical Society curator Michael Martins commented, "The idea that everyone must have been hot and irritable lent drama to the story."[18]

Scholars at the hundredth anniversary conference also discussed questions about Lizzie Borden's personality. Was she a cold-blooded murderer or a victim of her times? Just how peculiar was she?

"Virtually all books written about her are in agreement that she was strange," said keynote speaker Joyce G. Williams, an editor of *Lizzie Borden: A Case Book of Family and Crime in the 1890s.* "Some say *peculiar*, some say *sullen*, some say *in a trance, subject to fits, just out of it totally, incompatible with her family.* Today, we might say that she suffered from a personality disorder."[19]

Fellow scholar Gary Earl Russ spoke on the topic "If Lizzie Had Been Born 100 Years Later." Using his imagination to bring the Bordens into the twentieth century, Russ speculated that Andrew Borden would have shunned such modern innovations as push-button telephones and cable television. His sad and lonely wife would be a textbook example of chronic depression. Emma Borden would be a stay-at-home spinster despite the growing number of women in the workplace. Lizzie Borden, in turn, might tell her story on the *Oprah Winfrey* show. Once acquitted, she might show Barbara Walters and Connie Chung around Maplecroft, push for animal rights, and write a best-seller that would inevitably be turned into a movie.[20]

Although the tone of the conference was at times light-hearted, conferees said that they had come together to share scholarship—not to celebrate the murders. "How . . . do you celebrate a gruesome ax murder?" asked John L. Corrigan, Jr., a Fall River lawyer who served as chairman of the Legal and Forensics Panel.[21]

Soon after the conference, Bristol Community College professor Jules R. Ryckebusch launched *The Lizzie Borden Quarterly.* The first issue of the newsletter was dedicated to the Borden buffs of the world who inevitably needed to endure the odd looks of friends puzzled by their interest in a double homicide that occurred over one hundred years ago.[22]

Other Developments

Also around the time of the hundredth anniversary of the murders, the Springfield, Massachusetts, law firm founded by Lizzie Borden's attorney George Robinson considered releasing his papers from the case. After being advised by the Board of Bar Overseers to honor attorney-client confidentiality, the law firm decided against releasing the papers. In the 1998 case *Swidler and Berlin* v. *United States*, the United States Supreme Court, too, decided that attorney-client privilege extended after the death of a client.

Forensic scientist James Starrs, meanwhile, wanted to exhume (unbury) the bodies of Andrew and Abby Borden to perform tests on their remains. Many people in Fall River were outraged. Distant relatives pleaded for the Bordens to be allowed to rest in peace. The scientist reportedly honored their wishes.[23]

The Internet created a new forum for Lizzie buffs. "Lizzie Lives In Cyberspace!" one message declared.[24] Mystery buffs with the right computer equipment can log on to "The Virtual Lizzie Borden House" at <http://www.halfmoon.org/borden>.[25] Designer Nancy McNelly created a four-package program so viewers can choose either a two-dimensional or three-dimensional floorplan to solve the mystery.

Colleges throughout the United States use the Lizzie Borden case to teach history students how to do primary research by analyzing court transcripts and finding old town

This picture of Lizzie Borden was taken in 1905. Despite the fact that the trial ended in 1893 and Borden died in 1927, the case continues to draw interest.

records. On the other side of the world, students at the University of Singapore, too, can log onto the Internet to learn about the *Borden* case.

1990s Trials

In the 1990s, two sensational murder trials—O. J. Simpson's and nanny Louise Woodward's—prompted comparisons to the Lizzie Borden trial. Declared one headline on the Internet, "Lizzie Borden was the O. J. Simpson of her day."[26]

Similarities between the two cases abound. Both defendants paid for high-priced lawyers. O. J.'s lawyers emphasized the race of the defendant. Lizzie Borden's lawyers emphasized the gender of their defendant.[27] Neither defendant took the witness stand. Both were able to put the police and prosecutors on the defensive.[28] And, finally, both juries decided with remarkable speed to acquit. Despite modern-day fingerprinting and DNA analysis, the prosecutors in the *O. J. Simpson* case, too, failed to win a conviction.

In Massachusetts, a recent case compared to that of Lizzie Borden involved British nanny Louise Woodward, who was convicted of killing a baby in her care, but ultimately freed from prison by the judge. Her case prompted one pivotal lawmaker to vote against reinstating the death penalty, which Massachusetts had abolished in 1975. Like Lizzie Borden, Louise Woodward came across as someone who reminded the older men on the jury of their daughters during her trial.

"I would emphasize the fact that she was this round-faced, very girlish-looking girl, which I think matters a great deal," said Paula Fass, a professor at the University of California at Berkeley. "If she had been an older woman, it's certainly possible it would not have gone this way."[29]

At a mock trial at Stanford Law School in 1997 presided over by Supreme Court Justices William H. Rehnquist and Sandra Day O'Connor, Lizzie Borden once again was acquitted. The jury of law students did the best they could with the little they had. Once again, the jurors found reasonable doubt.

Some legal experts, though, say that courts today are more pro-government than they used to be. Lizzie Borden's self-incriminating inquest testimony would probably be admitted as evidence. Then again, a current-day lawyer might have advised her to remain silent in the first place.[30] Also, courts have become more skeptical about the supposed virtues of the upper classes.[31]

Fall River Today

Fall River continues to serve as a gathering place for Borden buffs. The old house on Second Street is now the Lizzie Borden Bed and Breakfast/Museum, with rooms restored to look like they did in August 1892. Visitors can stay in Lizzie's or Emma's bedroom, the Andrew and Abby Borden suite, the John V. Morse guest room, Bridget's attic room, or the two attic bedrooms named for lawyers in the case. Breakfast includes some of the same items the Bordens ate on that fateful day in August.

The Fall River Historical Society's Lizzie Borden collection also attracts numerous visitors. If not for Lizzie Borden, few people would have heard of Fall River. Although the historical society's museum shop sells Lizzie Borden plates, stationery, and calendars, it steers clear of merchandise it considers to be in poor taste.

Many people in Fall River, though, are clearly bothered by all the fuss about Lizzie Borden. Some dismiss talk by saying that Lizzie Borden was tried and acquitted and that they do not talk about it anymore. Others add that there is nothing left to the saga but hash and rehash.[32] Some residents of Fall River have come down with an acute case of Borden boredom.

The story, after all, has been told so many times that facts have become exaggerated into folklore. The "Forty Whacks" rhyme, in particular, has kept the legend alive. Through a hefty dose of fiction, real people become larger than life. Having a Victorian woman commit two unspeakable crimes makes for an interesting story.[33]

People accused of crimes are often less extraordinary in real life than in legend, however. As one observer speaking of legendary female criminals put it, "They are just average, every-day sort of women . . . in most instances they are futile ineffectual women who couldn't think of a better solution than to shoot their way out of a bad situation."[34] Thousands of women cope with similar problems in a more peaceful way, honoring the age-old commandment "Thou Shalt Not Kill."

Writers have long turned this age-old taboo into high

drama. In the Victorian era of strict morals, authors spun sensational tales of murder. Not surprisingly, the Victorian era gave rise to the modern detective story and the most famous literary detective of all—Sherlock Holmes.[35] More than one hundred years later, the Borden case has yet to be solved definitely. Few crime buffs can resist the challenge of an unsolved murder where they can throw themselves into the role of amateur detective.

Questions for Discussion

1. Imagine yourself in 1892 as an unmarried middle-class woman of thirty-two living in an unhappy family situation. What could you realistically do to improve your life? What kind of options would be available to you one hundred years later?

2. It is December 1892, and Alice Russell has just come forward with her story about the dress burning. Write an editorial about whether your opinion of Lizzie Borden has changed as a result of this new development.

3. You are the judge who needs to decide whether to include Lizzie Borden's testimony from the inquest. What would you decide?

4. Lawyers depending on circumstantial evidence try to develop a solid chain of events. How successful was the prosecution in the *Borden* case? Describe the strongest and weakest links in its case.

5. Lizzie Borden's defense attorney, former Massachusetts governor George Robinson, had appointed Associate Justice Justin Dewey to the bench. Do you think Judge Dewey should have been excused from the trial? Should judges who are friends or spouses of the attorneys be excused?

6. It is June 20, 1893, the final day of the *Borden* trial. Write an editorial either for or against the defendant.

7. As the principal of a middle school or high school, you notice children jumping rope to the Forty Whacks rhyme. ("Lizzie Borden took an axe / And gave her mother forty whacks / When she saw what she had done / She gave her father forty one.") What do you do?

8. You run a museum shop in Fall River and need to decide whether to carry merchandise such as plastic skeleton key chains, Lizzie Borden mugs, books depicting graphic details of the murders, and posters proclaiming Lizzie Borden as an American legend. What do you decide?

Chronology

September 13, 1822—Andrew J. Borden is born.

December 26, 1843—Andrew J. Borden marries Sarah A. Morse.

March 1, 1851—Emma Lenora Borden is born.

July 19, 1860—Lizzie Andrew Borden is born.

March 1863—Sarah Morse Borden dies

June 6, 1865—Andrew Borden marries Abby Durfee Gray.

1887—Whitehead property is purchased in Abby Borden's name; Lizzie Borden stops calling her stepmother "mother."

Tuesday, August 2–Wednesday, August 3, 1892—Andrew and Abby Borden are sick at midnight.

Wednesday, August 3, 1892 (the day before the murders):

- 9:00 A.M. Abby Borden visits Dr. Seabury Bowen.

- 10:00–11:30 A.M. Lizzie Borden allegedly tries to buy poison at a local drugstore.

- 1:30 P.M. John V. Morse arrives at Borden house.

- 7:00 P.M. Lizzie Borden visits her friend Alice Russell.

Thursday, August 4, 1892 (the day of the murders):

- 7:00–8:00 A.M. The elder Bordens, John V. Morse, and Bridget Sullivan eat breakfast.

- 8:55 A.M. Lizzie Borden comes downstairs.

- 9:30–10:30 A.M. Approximate time of Abby Borden's death.

- 11:00 A.M. Approximate time of Andrew Borden's death.

- 11:15 A.M. Police receive notification of disturbance at the Borden house.

Saturday, August 6, 1892 (two days after the murders):

- Funeral for Andrew and Abby Borden is held.

- The mayor of Fall River informs Lizzie Borden that she is a suspect in the murders of her father and stepmother.

Sunday, August 7, 1892—Alice Russell observes Lizzie Borden burning a dress at the kitchen stove.

Tuesday, August 9–Thursday, August 11, 1892:

- Judge Blaisdell conducts the inquest. Lizzie Borden gives her only testimony during the entire legal proceedings.

- Lizzie Borden is arrested for the murders of her father and stepmother.

August 12, 1892—Lizzie Borden is formally charged and pleads not guilty. She is taken to Taunton jail.

August 22–28, 1892—Preliminary hearing is held before Judge Blaisdell.

November 15–December 2, 1892—Grand Jury hears the case.

December 2, 1892—Lizzie Borden is charged with three counts of murder (one count for each of the murders, and one count for both murders combined).

June 5, 1893—The trial of Lizzie Borden begins.

June 20, 1893—Lizzie Borden is found not guilty.

1905—Emma Borden moves out of the home she shared with her sister, Lizzie, to settle in New Hampshire.

June 1, 1927—Lizzie Borden dies.

June 10, 1927—Emma Borden dies.

Chapter Notes

Chapter 1. A Terrible Crime

1. John U. Ayotte, "The Unfathomable Borden Riddle," *Yankee*, August 1966, p. 52.

2. Frank Spiering, *Lizzie* (New York: Random House, 1984), p. 21.

3. "Lizzie Borden: The Crime," DarkHorse Multimedia, Inc., 1998, <http://www.darkhorse.com/lizzie/lizziecrime.htm> (January 11, 1999).

4. Meyer Berger, "The Lizzie Borden Case," *The New York Times Magazine*, August 9, 1942, p. 26.

5. Russell Aiuto, "The Persistence of the Lizzie Borden Case in American Culture," n.d. <http:www.crimelibrary.com/lizzie/lizziemain.htm> (May 12, 1999).

6. Berger, p. 10.

7. Mary Cantwell, "Lizzie Borden Took an Ax," *The New York Times Magazine*, July 26, 1992, p. 20.

8. Edmund Pearson, *The Trial of Lizzie Borden* (Garden City, N.Y.: Doubleday, Doran & Company, Inc., 1937), p. 27.

9. Richard E. Rubenstein, ed., *Great Courtroom Battles*, Edgar Lustgarten, "The Lizzie Borden 'Axe Murder' Case" (Chicago: Playboy Press, 1973), p. 10.

10. Edward D. Radin, *Lizzie Borden: The Untold Story* (New York: Dell Publishing Co., 1961), p. 79.

11. Pearson, p. 166.

12. David Kent, *Forty Whacks* (Emmaus, Pa.: Yankee Books, 1992), p. 21.

13. Ibid.

Chapter 2. America in the 1890s

1. Kathryn Allamong Jacob, "She Couldn't Have Done It,

Even If She Did: Why Lizzie Borden Went Free," *American Heritage*, February 1978 , p. 49.

2. Joyce G. Williams, J. Eric Smithburn, and M. Jeanne Peterson, eds., *Lizzie Borden: A Case History of Family and Crime in the 1890s* (Bloomington, Ind.: T.I.S. Publications, 1980), p. 1.

3. N.A.F. McNelly, "The Borden Family," *The Virtual Lizzie Borden House*, 1996–1998, <http://www.halfmoon.org/borden/family.html> (January 1999).

4. Joan Hoff, *Law, Gender & Injustice: A Legal History of U.S. Women* (New York: New York University Press, 1991), p. 162.

5. Ibid., p. 169.

6. Samuel E. Sewall, *Legal Condition of Women in Massachusetts in 1886* (Boston: Addison C. Getchell, Book and Law Printer, 1886), p. 7.

7. Ralph Lindgren and Nadine Taub, ed., *The Law of Sex Discrimination,* Sarah Eisenstein, "Victorian Ideology and Working Women" (St. Paul, Minn.: West Publishing Co., 1988), p. 10.

8. Williams, p. 4.

9. Jacob, p. 49.

10. Ibid., p. 42.

11. McNelly, *The Virtual Lizzie Borden House*, <http://www.halfmoon.org/borden/family.html>.

12. Ann Schofield, "Lizzie Borden Took an Axe: History, Feminism and American Culture," *American Studies*, Spring 1993, p. 98.

13. Richard E. Rubenstein, ed., *Great Courtroom Battles*, Edgar Lustgarten, "The Lizzie Borden 'Axe Murder' Case" (Chicago: Playboy Press, 1973), p. 4.

14. McNelly, *The Virtual Lizzie Borden House*, <http://www.halfmoon.org/borden/family.html>.

15. Ibid.

16. Mary S. Hartman, "Borden, Lizzie," *The World Book Multimedia Encyclopedia* (Chicago: World Book, Inc., 1996).

17. Edmund Pearson, *The Trial of Lizzie Borden* (Garden City, N.Y.: Doubleday, Doran & Company, Inc., 1937), p. 8.

18. Jacob, p. 43.

19. Williams, p. 11.

20. Arnold R. Brown, *Lizzie Borden: The Legend, the Truth, the Final Chapter* (Nashville, Tenn.: TNL Rutledge Hill Press, 1991), p. 62.

21. Pearson, pp. 15–16.

22. Dorothy Dunbar, *Blood in the Parlor* (London: A. S. Barnes and Company, Inc., 1964), p. 35.

23. Pearson, p. 13.

24. Ibid., p. 22.

25. James W. Jeans, Sr., *Classics of the Courtroom: Highlights from the Commonwealth of Massachusetts v. Lizzie Borden* (Minnetonka, Minn.: The Professional Education Group, Inc., 1988), p. 45.

26. Williams, p. 28.

27. Jones, p. 219.

28. Brown, p. 100.

29. Robert Sullivan, *Goodbye Lizzie Borden* (Brattleboro, Vt.: The Stephen Greene Press, 1974), p. 37.

30. David Kent, *Forty Whacks* (Emmaus, Pa.: Yankee Books, 1992), p. 38.

31. Jacob, p. 49.

32. Frank Spiering, *Lizzie* (New York: Random House, 1984), p. 60.

33. Pearson, p. 30.

34. Kent, p. 50.

35. Ibid., p. 51.

36. Sullivan, p. 36.

37. Ibid, pp. 39–40; Kent, p. 43.

Chapter 3. The Case Begins

1. Victoria Lincoln, *A Private Disgrace: Lizzie Borden by Daylight* (New York: G.P. Putnam's Son, 1967), p. 109.

2. John H. Wigmore, "The Borden Case," *American Law Review*, 1893, p. 830.

3. Ibid., p. 831.

4. Robert Sullivan, *Goodbye Lizzie Borden* (Brattleboro, Vt.: The Stephen Greene Press, 1974), p. 43.

5. Lincoln, p. 167.

6. David Kent, *Forty Whacks* (Emmaus, Pa.: Yankee Books, 1992), p. 44.

7. Ann Jones, *Women Who Kill* (New York: Holt, Rinehart & Winston, 1980), p. 222.

8. Frank Spiering, *Lizzie* (New York: Random House, 1984), p. 78.

9. Kent, p. 48.

10. Anita Gustafson, *Guilty or Innocent?* (New York: Holt, Rinehart & Winston, 1985), p. 32.

11. "Inquest Testimony of Lizzie Borden," *New Bedford Evening Standard*, June 12, 1893. <http://web.meganet.net/digitech/LizzieBordenInquest.htm.> (March 15, 1999).

12. Ibid.

13. Lincoln, p. 65.

14. "Inquest Testimony of Lizzie Borden" <http://web.meganet.net/digitech/LizzieBordenInquest.htm>.

15. Ibid.

16. Ibid.

17. Ibid.

18. David Kent, in collaboration with Robert A. Flynn, *The Lizzie Borden Sourcebook* (Boston: Branden Publishing Company, 1992), p. 66.

19. Meyer Berger, "The Lizzie Borden Case," *The New York Times Magazine*, August 9, 1942, p. 27.

20. Kent and Flynn, p. 81.

21. Ibid., p. 63.

22. Ibid., p. 85.

23. Lincoln, p. 111.

24. Joyce G. Williams, J. Eric Smithburn, and M. Jeanne Peterson, eds., *Lizzie Borden: A Case History of Family and*

Crime in the 1890s (Bloomington, Ind.: T.I.S. Publications, 1980), p. 108.

25. Spiering, pp. 79–81.

26. Kent, p. 64.

27. Ibid., p. 67.

28. Edmund Pearson, *The Trial of Lizzie Borden* (Garden City, N.Y.: Doubleday, Doran & Company, Inc., 1937), p. 40.

29. Edward D. Radin, *Lizzie Borden: The Untold Story* (New York: Dell Publishing Co., Inc., 1961), p. 186.

30. Lincoln, p. 214.

31. Elwyn Jones, *On Trial: Seven Intriguing Cases of Capital Crime* (London: Macdonald and Jane's Publishers, Ltd., 1978), p. 29.

32. Gustafson, p. 33.

33. Williams, p. 131.

34. Kent, p. 74.

35. Pearson, pp. 160–161.

36. Spiering, p. 102.

37. Jones, pp. 235–236.

38. Kent, p. 76.

39. Jones, p. 228.

40. Kent, pp. 76–77.

41. Ibid., pp. 77–78.

42. Jones, p. 217.

43. Radin, p. 103.

44. Michael Martins and Dennis A. Binette, eds., *The Commonwealth of Massachusetts vs. Lizzie A. Borden: The Knowlton Papers, 1892–1893* (Fall River, Mass.: The Fall River Historical Society, 1994), p. 158.

45. Sullivan, p. 73.

46. Jones, p. 236.

47. Spiering, p. 107.

48. Ibid., p. 108.

49. Sullivan, p. 204.

Chapter 4. The Case Against Lizzie Borden

1. Edward D. Radin, *Lizzie Borden: The Untold Story* (New York: Dell Publishing Co., Inc., 1961), p. 106.

2. Robert Sullivan, *Goodbye Lizzie Borden* (Brattleboro, Vt.: The Stephen Greene Press, 1974), pp. 74–75; Ann Jones, *Women Who Kill* (New York: Holt, Rinehart & Winston, 1980), p. 217.

3. Edmund Pearson, ed., *The Trial of Lizzie Borden* (Garden City, N.Y.: Doubleday, Doran & Company, Inc., 1937), p. 106.

4. Richard E. Rubenstein, ed., *Great Courtroom Battles*, Edgar Lustgarten, "The Lizzie Borden 'Axe Murder' Case" (Chicago: Playboy Press, 1973), pp. 13–14.

5. Radin, p. 111.

6. Pearson, p. 232.

7. Joyce G. Williams, J. Eric Smithburn, and M. Jeanne Peterson, eds., *Lizzie Borden: A Case History of Family and Crime in the 1890s* (Bloomington, Ind.: T.I.S. Publications, 1980), p. 141.

8. Anita Gustafson, *Guilty or Innocent?* (New York: Holt, Rinehart & Winston, 1985), p. 35; Meyer Berger, "The Lizzie Borden Case," *The New York Times Magazine*, August 9, 1942, p. 26.

9. Sullivan, p. 101.

10. Ibid.

11. Frank Spiering, *Lizzie* (New York: Random House, 1984), p. 134; Williams, p. 154.

12. Sullivan, p. 126.

13. Ibid., p. 130.

14. Ibid., p. 131.

15. Williams, p. 187.

16. Sullivan, p. 163.

17. Williams, p. 170.

18. Ibid., p. 172.

19. Sullivan, p. 197.

20. Spiering, p. 148.; Victoria Lincoln, *A Private Disgrace: Lizzie Borden by Daylight* (New York: G.P. Putnam's Sons, 1967), p. 139.

21. Spiering, p. 149.

22. Rubenstein, p. 24.

23. Pearson, p. 327.

24. Ann Jones, *Women Who Kill* (New York: Holt, Rinehart & Winston, 1980), p. 222.

25. John H. Wigmore, "The Borden Case," *American Law Review*, 1893, p. 837.

26. Ibid.

27. Ibid., p. 838.

28. Spiering, p. 170.

Chapter 5. Defending Lizzie Borden

1. Richard E. Rubenstein, ed., *Great Courtroom Battles*, Edgar Lustgarten, "The Lizzie Borden 'Axe Murder' Case" (Chicago: Playboy Press, 1973), p. 24.

2. Joyce G. Williams, J. Eric Smithburn, and M. Jeanne Peterson, eds., *Lizzie Borden: A Case History of Family and Crime in the 1890s* (Bloomington, Ind.: T.I.S. Publications, 1980), p. 134.

3. Ann Jones, *Women Who Kill* (New York: Holt, Rinehart & Winston, 1980), pp. 222–223.

4. Ibid., p. 225.

5. Robert Sullivan, *Goodbye Lizzie Borden* (Brattleboro, Vt.: The Stephen Greene Press, 1974), p. 180.

6. James W. Jeans, Sr., *Classics of the Courtroom: Highlights from The Commonwealth of Massachusetts v. Lizzie Borden* (Minnetonka, Minn.: The Professional Education Group, Inc., 1988), p. 75.

7. Ibid.

8. Jeans, p. 84.

9. Ibid., p. 87.

10. Ibid.

11. Edmund Pearson, *The Trial of Lizzie Borden* (Garden City, N.Y.: Doubleday, Doran & Company, Inc., 1937), p. 152.

12. Radin, p. 126

13. Pearson, p. 162.

14. Frank Spiering, *Lizzie* (New York: Random House, 1984), p. 139.

15. Radin, p. 144.

16. Ibid., p. 145.

17. Arnold R. Brown, *Lizzie Borden: The Legend, the Truth, the Final Chapter* (Nashville, Tenn.: TNL Rutledge Hill Press, 1991), p. 261.

18. Ibid.

19. Sullivan, p. 154.

20. David Kent, *Forty Whacks* (Emmaus, Pa.: Yankee Books, 1992), p. 161.

21. Rubenstein, p. 25.

22. Jeans, pp. 147–148.

23. Ibid., p. 159.

24. Ibid., p. 273.

25. Sullivan, p. 167.

26. Kent, p. 171.

27. Jeans, p. 226.

28. Ibid., p. 205.

29. Sullivan, p. 168.

30. Jeans, p. 229.

31. Ibid., p. 230.

32. Spiering, p. 168.

33. Rubenstein, p. 28.

Chapter 6. The Decision

1. Edmund Pearson, *The Trial of Lizzie Borden* (Garden City, N.Y.: Doubleday, Doran & Company, Inc., 1937), p. 377.

2. Robert Sullivan, *Goodbye Lizzie Borden* (Brattleboro, Vt.: The Stephen Greene Press, 1974), p. 172.

3. Joyce G. Williams, J. Eric Smithburn, and M. Jeanne Peterson, eds., *Lizzie Borden: A Case History of Family and Crime in the 1890s* (Bloomington, Ind.: T.I.S. Publications, 1980) p. 210.

4. James W. Jeans, Sr., *Classics of the Courtroom: Highlights from The Commonwealth of Massachusetts v. Lizzie Borden*

(Minnetonka, Minn.: The Professional Education Group, Inc., 1988), p. 280.

5. Sullivan, p. 175.

6. Jeans, pp. 298–299.

7. David Kent in collaboration with Robert A. Flynn, *The Lizzie Borden Sourcebook* (Boston: Branden Publishing Company, 1992), p. 307.

8. Kathryn Allamong Jacob, "She Couldn't Have Done It, Even If She Did: Why Lizzie Borden Went Free," *American Heritage*, January 1978, p. 52.

9. Sullivan, p. 178.

10. Kent and Flynn, p. 313.

11. Ibid., p. 307.

12. Williams, p. 228.

13. Ibid., p. 229.

14. Ibid.

15. Sullivan, p. 179.

16. Williams, p. 230.

17. Kent and Flynn, p. 328.

18. Edward D. Radin, *Lizzie Borden: The Untold Story* (New York: Dell Publishing Co., Inc., 1961), p. 225.

19. Sullivan, p. 205.

20. Ibid., p. 199.

21. John H. Wigmore, "The Borden Case," *American Law Review*, 1893, p. 835.

22. Kent and Flynn, p. 355.

23. Frank Spiering, *Lizzie* (New York: Random House, 1984), p. 184.

24. Author telephone interview with Michael Martins, May 18, 1999.

25. Kent and Flynn, p. 232.

26. Jules R. Ryckebusch, ed., *Proceedings: Lizzie Borden Conference*; John David Marshall, "Librarians in the Life and Legend of Lizzie Borden" (Portland, Maine: King Philip Publishing, Co., 1993), p. 313.

27. Williams, p. 235.

The Lizzie Borden "Axe Murder" Trial

28. Dorothy Dunbar, *Blood in the Parlor* (London: A. S. Barnes and Company, Inc., 1964), p. 26.

29. Spiering, p. 209.

30. Kent and Flynn, p. 329.

31. David Wallechinsky and Irving Wallace, *The People's Almanac #2* (New York: William Morrow and Company, Inc., 1978), p. 500.

32. Radin, p. 229.

33. Kent and Flynn, p. 331.

34. Radin, p. 236.

35. Williams, p. 248.

36. Ibid., p. 252.

37. Ibid.

38. Ibid., p. 253.

39. Ibid., p. 262.

40. Spiering, p. 226.

Chapter 7. The Continuing Fascination

1. Edward D. Radin, *Lizzie Borden: The Untold Story* (New York: Dell Publishing Co., Inc., 1961), p. 105.

2. Robert Sullivan, *Goodbye Lizzie Borden* (Brattleboro, Vt.: The Stephen Greene Press, 1974), p. 1.

3. Kathleen M. Heide, *Why Kids Kill Parents: Child Abuse and Adolescent Homicide* (Columbus: Ohio State University Press, 1992), p. 3.

4. Sullivan, p. 1.

5. Anthony Boucher, ed., *The Quality of Murder*, James Reach, "The Myth of Lizzie Borden" (New York: E.P. Dutton & Co., Inc., 1962), p. 60.

6. Ibid., p. 61.

7. Boucher, p. 62.

8. Ibid.

9. David Kent in collaboration with Robert A. Flynn, *The Lizzie Borden Sourcebook* (Boston: Branden Publishing Company, 1992), p. 348.

10. Ann Jones, *Women Who Kill* (New York: Holt, Rinehart & Winston, 1980), p. 237.

11. Robert A. Flynn, *The Borden Murders: An Annotated Bibliography* (Portland, Maine: King Philip Publishing Co.), pp. 9–10.

12. Radin, p. 218.

13. Boucher, p. 59.

14. David Gates, "A New Whack at the Borden Case," *Newsweek*, June 4, 1984, p. 12.

15. Author telephone interview with Bruce Laurie, May 24, 1999.

16. Kent and Flynn, bookjacket.

17. Jules R. Ryckebusch, ed., *Proceedings: Lizzie Borden Conference*, William L. Masterson, "The Borden Case; Myths vs. Facts" (Fall River, Mass.: Bristol Community College; Portland, Maine: King Philip Publishing, Co., 1993), p. 199.

18. Author telephone interview with Michael Martins, May 18, 1999.

19. Ryckebusch, Joyce G. Williams, "Keynote Address," pp. 8–9.

20. Ibid.

21. Mary Cantwell, "Lizzie Borden Took an Ax," *The New York Times Magazine*, July 26, 1992, p. 43.

22. Kenneth J. Souza, "The Editor's Verdict," *The Lizzie Borden Quarterly*, January 1993, p. 3.

23. Author telephone interview with Michael Martins, May 18, 1999.

24. Ed Sams, *Lizzie Borden Unlocked!* © 1998, <http://www.curiouschapbooks.com/trialsoflb.htm> (April 26, 2000).

25. N.A.F. McNelly, *The Virtual Lizzie Borden House*, 1996–1998 <http://www.halfmoon.org/borden/family.html> (March 15, 1999).

26. Ibid.

27. Ibid.

28. William J. Eaton, "Just Like O. J.'s Trial, But Without Kato," *American Journalism Review*, December 1995, p. 12.

29. Carey Goldberg. "A Further Distinction for the Au Pair," *The New York Times*, November 13, 1997, p. 14.

30. Marijke Rijsberman, "Lizzie Borden Today, Lizzie Borden Acquitted Again," © 1999, <http://lawschool.stanford.edu/campaign/lizzie/sept.html> (March 15, 1999).

31. Dorothy Dunbar, *Blood in the Parlor* (London: A. S. Barnes and Company, Inc., 1964), p. 45.

32. Gates, p. 12.

33. Boucher, p. 64.

34. Jones, p. 14.

35. William H. Harris and Judith S. Levey, *The New Columbia Encyclopedia*, "Detective Story" (New York: Columbia University Press, 1975), pp. 752–753.

Glossary

acquitted—Pronounced not guilty of the crime charged.

alibi—A claim to have been elsewhere when the crime in question was committed.

axe or ax—A cutting tool or weapon with a heavy-bladed head attached to a handle. (*See* hatchet.)

bail—The system allowing for the temporary release of a prisoner awaiting trial in exchange for money.

circumstantial evidence—Details that seem to point to a conclusion but are not absolute.

district attorney—The prosecutor for the local area.

grand jury—A judicial body that examines the evidence against a suspect to determine whether a case should be dismissed or tried before a judge and/or jury.

hatchet—An axe with a short handle for use by one hand.

indictment—A formal criminal charge against a suspect.

inquest—A legal procedure used to gather information.

marshal—A high officer in the police, military, or judicial system.

mutton—An inexpensive cut of meat from a grown sheep rather than a young lamb.

probable cause—Reasonable grounds for believing that the person on trial is guilty of the crime charged.

prosecutor—The attorney who conducts criminal cases on behalf of the state or the people.

prussic acid—A poisonous colorless liquid with the smell of peach blossoms or bitter almonds.

settlement house—A community center for the neighborhood poor.

suffragists—Supporters of a woman's right to vote.

Victorian era—The time from 1837 to 1901 when Queen Victoria ruled over Great Britain.

Further Reading

Flynn, Robert A. *The Borden Murders: An Annotated Bibliography.* Portland, Maine: King Philip Publishing Company, 1992.

Kent, David in collaboration with Robert A. Flynn. *The Lizzie Borden Sourcebook.* Boston: Branden Publishing Company, Inc., 1992.

Levinson, Nancy Smiler. *Turn of the Century.* New York: Lodestar Books, 1994.

Ohrn, Deborah G., ed. *Herstory.* New York: Viking Penguin, 1999.

Rappaport, Doreen. *The Lizzie Borden Trial.* New York: Harper Collins Publishers, 1992.

Internet Addresses

Ed Sams, *Lizzie Borden Unlocked*, Yellow Tulip Press, 1996–1999. <http://www.curiouschapbooks.com/cntnts.html>

Fall River Police Department Homepage. "Lizzie Borden's Hometown PD." n.d. <http://www.frpd.org>

N.A.F. McNelly, *The Virtual Lizzie Borden House*, 1996–1998. <http://www.halfmoon.org/borden>

Russell Aiuto, *Lizzie Borden.* <http://www.crimelibrary.com/lizzie/lizziemain.htm>

Index

release of his case papers
considered, 100
Russell, Alice,
morning murders are
discovered, 7, 8
talk of poison with Abby
Borden, 21

S
Stone, Lucy, 47
Sullivan, Maggie,
life after Borden case, 89–90
letters urging arrest of, 26
morning murders are
discovered, 7, 23
testimony at the inquest, 33
testimony at trial, 52

T
trial
choosing jury, 46–47

closing arguments, 61–63,
74–78
defense victories, 71–72
judge's plea for innocent verdict,
81
verdict, 80, 81
Trickey, Henry, 44–45
Twain, Mark, 14

V
Victorian era, 14
Victorian women, 16, 17

W
Whitehead, Sarah, 19
Women's Christian Temperance
Union, 90–91
women's right to vote, 16
Wood, Dr. Edward S., 55–56